LEADING YOUR
ORGANIZATION TO
HIGH PERFORMANCE

LEADING YOUR ORGANIZATION TO HIGH PERFORMANCE:

A GUIDE FOR EXECUTIVES

A. Lad Burgin

To my sons, Jason and Gregory, who are continuing sources of inspiration to me.

Contents

Acknowledgements

Any project, such as writing this book, is a challenge. It reflects more than forty years of my professional experience. I would like to acknowledge the contributions of a few key people. First is Professor Robert Miljus who started me on this path. Next is Jerry Stilson who was an exceptional mentor and taught me a great deal about leadership as we campaigned his sloop, the Windancer, in the Great Lakes sail racing circuit. John O'Neil, colleague, good friend and published author, provided inspiration and support. John O'Callaghan, friend and exceptional executive, who has engaged with me in many dialogues about leadership and organizational effectiveness and provided feedback on the manuscript. My colleagues and friends Theresa Ruby and Ross Gray of Global House Consulting for their thoughtful reading of the manuscript and cogent feedback. Barbara Fandrich who applied her superb editorial skills. Finally, to my son, Jason, who was always ready to read what I had written and provide enthusiastic support for the project.

Chapter 1:
A Life's Work

It was a Wednesday morning. I was sitting in a conference room at my client's office waiting for him to join me. My client, Grant, was the lead director of a publicly traded medical devices company, Gynecare, Inc. (GI) and a partner in a leading venture capital firm.

I had been retained by Grant ninety days earlier to work with the management team at the company. I was there to tell him he needed to replace the chief executive officer.

The door opened, he walked in, said hello, and in the same breath he said, "We need to get a new CEO for GI." I said, "That's interesting because that is what I came to tell you this morning."

I had not heard any financial news that morning. It turns out that the lead analyst who covered GI's stock had come out with a highly negative report, cutting GI's rating from Buy to Sell. The stock had tanked at the opening of the market, losing a substantial portion of its market value.

After a brief conversation about what I had found at GI, Grant asked, "What time can you be here this afternoon?" At 4:00 pm, he introduced me to the management team as the new CEO. I will share more about this experience as this story progresses.

My career passion is business performance, specifically creating and sustaining high performance over time in the face of change and competition in the business environment. Over the past forty-plus years, I have pursued this interest as a business executive and a consultant to business executives.

I have had the good fortune to be a corporate staff executive in a large corporation, the CEO of three new business startups, and the CEO of a publicly traded company. As a consultant, I have worked with the CEOs of more than 300 companies in twenty-five different industries around the world. As a board member, I have served on the boards of five corporations and consulted with many more.

My purpose in writing this book is to share with you what I have learned about creating and sustaining high performance. In a world characterized by hyper-competition, rapid technological change, and globalization, I have come to believe that building a high-performance organization is one of the few ways to create a sustainable competitive advantage.

It is clear to me that executive leadership is the key element that underlies any organization's long-term effectiveness and performance. After all my years of experience with executive leadership, I am still amazed at the impact that one person in a key executive role can have on an organization.

It takes energy to be an effective leader. You must develop and maintain the capacity to lead. You must be physically, mentally, and emotionally available. High-capacity leaders are focused, act purposefully to address situations, and set the positive example required to maintain the performance of an organization. Leaders who allow themselves to become tired or overly stressed become reactive, lose focus, and have difficulty enacting and sustaining the daily behavior required to lead effectively.

The path to effective leadership involves developing a leadership practice to sustain the capacity to lead in the face of the many challenges that come along from day to day. I will return to the critical issue of sustaining the capacity to lead in the closing chapter.

When I started my career, I was interested in developing products. My interest in high performance was captured by an early business experience with a company that had attained the leadership position in its industry and then fell by the wayside due to its inability to respond quickly and forcefully to changes in its market.

A Business Experience That Changed My Life

The story begins in the spring of 1967. I had come to The Ohio State University in 1963 to play football for the legendary coach Woody Hayes, who was as intent to see his players receive a good education as he was to win football games.

Despite much advice to the contrary, I had chosen to pursue a double major in mechanical engineering and business. Thus, I found myself at the end of my athletic scholarship with one year of academic work to complete to graduate. Good fortune smiled upon me and I found a well-paying, part-time job as a design draftsman in the product development group of a local industrial products company. My experience over the next two-and-a-half years changed my life and set my career on the path I have pursued for more than forty years.

The company, Dennison Engineering, had been run by its founder for many years. Under his stewardship, the company had become a leader in its industry of fluid power components and systems. Shortly before I arrived at the company, the founder sold the business to a big, East Coast–based conglomerate.

As the newest and most junior person on the product development staff, one of my key job duties was to be the "go for" for the department. Daily, I was dispatched to all areas of the product development laboratory and the two manufacturing facilities on all kinds of errands that usually involved either delivering something or picking something up. The "go for" was a great job. I probably got to know and talk to more people throughout the company than anyone else.

I soon found I had arrived at a particularly interesting point in the company's history. The company was in the midst of two big and fundamental changes. First, the transition from the founder's leadership of a freestanding company to a division in a multi-division company was still underway. Second, there was a fundamental shift in the fluid power market.

A Change in Leadership

Mr. Dennison, the founder, had built up the business over many years. In the early days, he designed, built, sold, and serviced the products himself. The company prospered and became the leader in its industry.

The founder was a legend when I arrived. He had been well-known, respected, and loved throughout the company. He had run the business decisively and with a firm hand. He also had a great capacity with people and knew most of the employees by their first name. He spent time on the factory floor almost every day. People felt he was fair, and most important, he would listen to people's ideas and advice.

After the sale of the company, a "professional manager" was sent from the parent company to succeed the founder. The new Division President had been in place for about a year. He was a mystery to most of the people in the company. He stayed in his office or traveled to the East Coast for meetings. People noticed that their managers seemed to be much more stressed since his arrival and he was reported to have "aggressive" goals for the Division.

The Division President seemed to be oblivious to the impact he was having on the managers and employees. It was my first experience with a leadership transition in the process of going bad. I will have more to say about this later.

A Change in the Market

The traditional market for the company's products had been in stationary applications like factory assembly lines, cranes, and hoists. This market had matured, and the company enjoyed a dominant market position. Its products were of high quality, extremely reliable, built to last 100 years and priced to reflect these attributes. If one ever did break down, a loner product was shipped to the customer; the customer would ship the failed product back to the factory where it was rebuilt and sent back to the customer who would ship the loaner product back.

In the latter part of the 1960s, the fluid power market was going mobile. The emerging market was for hydraulic components and systems to go into trucks, construction equipment, airplanes, and other mobile applications. The equipment manufacturers wanted components and systems that were scaled to work on this equipment and reasonably (low) priced. The end users wanted components that would work reliably for a fixed life. When a component broke or wore out, they wanted to have a relatively unskilled maintenance person be able to quickly remove the component in the field, throw it away and replace it with a new one. They also wanted quick delivery of replacement components so they would not have to keep a large inventory of them.

The Mobile Product Line

I arrived in the middle of an intensive effort to develop a new line of products for the mobile market. Several of the company's competitors had successfully brought out products for the new market. With every day that went by, the company was giving this new market away to its competitors.

The product development effort had been underway for more than a year. The marketing people had done a great job understanding the needs of customers and end users and creating clear specifications. The product development people had completed designs for the new product lines and were building and testing prototypes. Over the next nine months, the prototypes were tested, refined, and field-tested. At last, they were passed to manufacturing to get them into production.

What happened next was a heartrending saga to any businessperson. The designs for the new products went into manufacturing engineering. The people in manufacturing engineering, who had spent their careers building the 100-year, lifetime products, went to work on the new product line. Three months passed, then six months, then nine months. Finally, a full year after the new product line was handed off to manufacturing the first new products started to emerge. Much to the horror of the marketing and product development people, the new products had been reengineered to look surprisingly like the old products. The manufacturing engineers just could not bring themselves to put "flimsy" products into the market.

It was my first experience with a broken business process and the difficulties of major organizational change.

The Bottom Line

The result is not hard to guess. It took the company another year to get the mobile products into the marketplace. By that time, the competition had won the game and staked out their leadership positions.

The home office in the east had become worried about the company's performance and the Division President was feeling the pressure, which he passed on to management who passed it on to the employees.

Just as the company was finally bringing its products to market, the employees revolted. A union organizing drive was started, an election was held, the union won, and the operations were shut down by a bitter and prolonged strike!

By this time, I had earned my bachelor's degree and an MBA. It had been fascinating to be working in a live business that was wrestling with the real-life problems of leadership, organizational change, and adapting to fundamental change in its business environment. The experience kindled an interest in organizational effectiveness and performance that has stayed with me to this day.

Creating a Sustainable Competitive Advantage

Look around the world of business and you will see many stories of businesses that either never got off the ground or businesses that attained leadership positions in their industries, like the fluid power company, and then faltered when market changes occurred. Even the biggest and best companies, such as IBM, Ford, and Hewlett Packard, have been through the experience of falling from prominence. See

Mr. Lou Gerstner's wonderful book[1] for a great account of how IBM ascended to prominence during the mainframe era, lost its leadership position when the desktop revolution swept through the computer industry, and regained its leadership with the advent of the Internet and global networking. IBM then fell behind once more and is currently staging a resurgence in the world of services, cloud computing, big data, and artificial intelligence.

Building a business into a leadership position and sustaining leadership over time is one of the most challenging missions that can be undertaken. It is a lot like winning the national championship in college football. Once you have done it, you can be sure you will get every team's best game when you play them. Knocking the leader off is a highly motivating goal in both football and business.

In today's business world, it is exceedingly difficult to find sources of sustainable advantage. The best technology is no guarantee of success. Myriad examples abound of superior technologies that lost out to lesser technologies coupled to superior marketing or execution. Beta lost to VHS in video. Informix lost to Oracle in databases. Blackberry lost to Android and Apple. Tribe Networks and My Space lost to Facebook in social networks. Many established retailers have lost to Amazon.

To win consistently, a business must do many things well to out- execute its competition and create value for its customers and investors. It must:

- Attract and retain great talent

---

[1] Gerstner, Louis V., Jr. *Who Says Elephants Can't Dance?* New York: Harper Collins Publishers, 2002.

- Understand its customers and its competitors and be driven by quality and customer service

- Have a clear strategic focus

- Adapt quickly, redeploying resources to take advantage of trends and opportunities in its business environment

- Innovate in both its internal processes and its products and services

- Be structured, networked and effectively integrated by culture, business processes, and management systems so the knowledge and skills that people possess can be quickly and effectively mobilized to solve problems

- Create and sustain a learning environment in which employees can continuously reskill and improve themselves to keep up with the high rate of change characteristic of the world today

In short, to win consistently in business, or sports, requires a high-performance organization. It requires an environment in which people with diverse needs, preferences, values, and capabilities work effectively together to set and achieve goals. It must be a place in which people focus their energy and creativity on superior performance in a context of learning. Lester Thurow, past dean of the MIT Business School, has captured this eloquently:

Knowledge employed through the skills of people has become the only source of long-run sustainable advantage.[2]

As have business executive Larry Bossidy and strategy consultant Ram Charan:

An organization's human beings are its most reliable resource for generating excellent results year after year. Their judgments, experiences and capabilities make the difference between success and failure.[3]

A high-performance organization is difficult to create and once created it is hard to duplicate. Therein lies the sustainable, competitive advantage.

Who is responsible for building a high-performance organization? It's the CEO; it's his or her job, isn't it?

The Power of Executive Leadership

Executive leadership is the key factor that drives an organization's effectiveness and performance. After more than forty years of experience with executive leadership, I am still amazed at the impact one person in a key executive role can have on an organization.

One has only to look at the impact of Lou Gerstner at IBM, Larry Bossidy at Allied Signal, Steve Jobs at Apple, or Alan Mulally at Boeing and Ford, to see how a highly capable executive can restore a sick business to health. On the other hand, instances such as Enron, J.C. Penney, Tyco, AGI, and

---

[2] Thurow, Lester. *The Future of Capitalism*. New York: William Morrow and Company, 1996.

[3] Bossidy, Larry and Charan, Ram. *Execution: The Discipline of Getting Things Done*. New York: Crown Business, 2002.

Lehman Brothers show us how disastrous incapable executives can be for a corporation and its employees, shareholders, suppliers, and customers.

Two of the best illustrations of the importance and impact of executive leadership are the very fine research programs carried out by Jim Collins and presented in his two exceptional books, *Built to Last* and *Good to Great*.[4] [5]

In *Built to Last*, Jim reported on his research on companies that rose to prominence in their industries and then sustained their industry leadership. These companies far outperformed comparison companies in their own industries. In *Good to Great*, Jim repeated his research with a group of companies that were able to transform themselves and distance themselves from their competitors. The companies, which made the jump from good to great, significantly outperformed comparison companies in their industries.

In both of these investigations, the role of executive leadership was prominent. In the "Built to Last" companies, each had one or more highly capable CEOs who focused and led their companies to prominence in their industries. In the "Good to Great" companies, CEOs possessing superior leadership capabilities designed and executed strategies and operational plans that resulted in their companies substantially outperforming their competitors. Great companies result from great leadership!

How does a CEO build a high-performance organization?

---

[4] Collins, James C. *Good to Great*. New York: Harper Collins Publishers, 2001.

[5] Collins, James C. and Porras, Jerry I. *Built to Last*. New York: Harper Collins Publishers, 1994.

Building a High-Performance Organization

A high-performance organization produces sustained, long-term performance. Its financial, product and service quality, and customer service results are consistently superior to its competitors. It anticipates and adapts quickly to changes and trends in its business environment. It innovates in both the products and services it provides to its customers and its internal processes and practices. Its internal effectiveness and efficiency allow it to use speed as a competitive weapon. It continuously improves.

Building a high-performance organization is an arduous journey. It requires thinking and working with a complex social system. The path for this journey encompasses:

- Strategic leadership

- Superior customer experience

- Clear strategic focus

- Effective structure and networks

- Highly capable people who possess the right competencies

- Corporate culture that supports high performance

- Highly effective unit and team leadership

- Appropriately designed jobs, roles, and assignments

- Effective and efficient management systems and business processes to focus on results

- Sustaining the capacity to lead over the long-term

The key to building a high-performance organization is executive leadership.

Chapter 2:
Strategic Leadership

The process of building and sustaining a high-performance company requires a high level of leadership capability. Jim Collins uses the name "Level 5 Leadership."[6] Larry Bossidy and Ram Charan focus on highly effective executive leadership.[7] Lou Gerstner emphasizes superior executive leadership.[8]

I prefer the term **strategic leadership** because it emphasizes what is required to create high performance. The CEO and the senior team are responsible for the strategic health of the business. **Strategic health** is an organizational state in which short and long-term goals, objectives, and actions are balanced and adaptability, innovation, continuous learning and improvement, and speed are pursued as paths to superior results.[9] It is the process of attracting, energizing, focusing, aligning, and retaining people to accomplish results and build a highly effective organization.

The CEO or division general manager is the key. His or her values and daily behavior create the environment for the senior team. He or she selects the members of the senior team either by recruiting and hiring them, or by retaining them in their positions.

[6] Collins, Jim. *Good to Great*, p.17.

[7] Bossidy, Larry and Charan, Ram. *Execution: The Discipline of Getting Things Done*, p.24.

[8] Gerstner, Louis V., Jr. *Who Says Elephants Can't Dance?* p.235.

[9] Burgin, A. Lad and Koss, Ellee. *Transformation to High Performance*, p.10.

A leader who is trying to build a high-performance organization needs to start by taking stock of himself and the members of the senior team. He must understand himself well and be aware of his own values and capabilities and how they impact his daily behavior as a leader. Also, he must understand the values, capabilities, and daily behaviors of the members of the senior team.

Daily behavior is the currency of leadership. Through daily behavior, a leader creates the environment that determines the focus, motivation, and performance of the people on which the success of an organization depends.

I have had the good fortune to work with great leaders and to practice strategic leadership myself as a CEO. Out of these experiences, I have developed a keen appreciation for the practice of leadership.

The key leader sets the tone of the organization through his or her daily leadership behavior. Building and sustaining high performance requires the key leader to be proficient at the following tasks:

- Leading the company

- Working with a team

- Establishing and communicating direction

- Aligning people with the direction

- Developing managers and leaders

- Empowering, supporting, and motivating people

- Identifying and making tough decisions

- Keeping him/herself mentally and physically fit to lead

These are the tasks of strategic leadership.

Leading the Company

Start with yourself. Your top priority is to be an effective leader. Be aware that you are constantly "on stage," being observed by managers and employees. **Your daily behavior is the key to your effectiveness as a leader**. Conscious awareness that your daily behavior has the strongest impact on what happens in the company over time will cause you to behave in a purposeful way.

Try to handle the many small situations that occur on a daily basis by acting rather than reacting. Be aware that your handling of even small situations with your direct reports and others has a significant impact on how people do their jobs.

Try to set a positive example in your actions. The best leaders I have worked with do this by treating each person with whom they interact with respect and dignity. Every transaction is important. A worthy goal is to have each person that you communicate with leave the interaction with a feeling that they are important to you and to the success of the company. Take the time to get to know people. Ask them for input, listen to what they have to say, and express your appreciation for their input and efforts.

Place a high value on personal integrity. Be careful to act with integrity in your dealings with others. Try to be honest and candid in your interactions with everyone. Take the time to explain the reasons for your decisions and invite questions about issues and give direct answers. If you can't answer directly due to confidentiality, clearly state that you are not able to discuss the issue at the time.

Be serious about commitments. Keep commitments, even in small matters such as starting meetings on time and responding to email and telephone calls. Avoid making commitments that you can't fulfill. Good intentions that aren't fulfilled erode your credibility as a leader.

Make a conscious effort to remain calm in times of stress. Anxiety and fear are enemies of teamwork and effective decision-making.

It is important to manage your own anxiety and reduce the anxiety of individuals and teams when the heat is on.

Be decisive. Decisions must be made and followed through. Use participation to involve others and build commitment to decisions. You do not need to make all the decisions yourself. Try to be sensitive to accord others the ownership of specific decisions. However, be clear that decisions must be made in a timely manner and don't allow them to slide.

Assembling, Building, and Working with a Team

Return with me to the GI story from page 1.

Wednesday 4:15. My client leaves the room and there I am with the members of the management team. Fortunately, I'd had ninety days of experience with them leading up to this day.

I started out by saying, "As we all know, this company is in trouble and it is now our job to fix it."

At some point you will be faced with the challenge of taking a group of executives and developing them into an effective management team. When you are, a good place to start is to meet with your direct reports in a group setting. Begin the meeting by explaining your expectations of the executive team. Tell them that, from this moment on, you expect them to work together with you to identify and solve the company's problems and execute its business plan.

Explain that you expect it will take some time for all of you to learn to work together as an effective team. Ask each member of the group to place working as an effective team member as their number one objective and state that teamwork will be a key criterion in evaluating their performance. Emphasize that, in addition to teamwork at the executive level, you expect each member of the executive team to actively foster teamwork in the company.

Wednesday 4:35. I stopped talking and asked the group if there were any questions or comments. Silence reigned! I then asked the team members to make a commitment to work with me to turn the company around. I then went around the room member by member and asked if they would commit to this mission. Each of them said yes, so I said, "Let's get to work" and concluded the meeting.

Thursday 7:30 am. I walked into my new office and started the adventure of restoring GI to good health. What to do with the first sixty days?

Are there any tough challenges standing in the way? My management team was a mess. The members were all experienced and capable people, but they just did not get along. One of the vice presidents was an outcast. He had been hired over the objections of two other VPs and their approach was to avoid him and not include him whenever possible. Two other VPs would get into open and severe conflict in team meetings and sometimes in the open office.

Disagreement and conflict among team members is healthy to a point. It brings out points of view, raises issues and generates productive dialogue. Beyond a certain point, conflict becomes destructive. This one was destructive and having a negative impact on the company.

When you encounter these types of situations, the answer is to sit down with the people involved and make it perfectly clear their behavior is <u>inappropriate and unacceptable.</u> Then make it perfectly clear how you expect them to behave going forward. In this case, I was clear that if things did not change, either one, or both, would be asked to leave the company.

Once you have addressed any of these challenges, plan and implement an offsite meeting for the executive team to go over every aspect of the company's operations. A professional facilitator can be a great asset here. Following the meeting, establish regular weekly executive team meetings to follow up on the list of action items and to engage the team in problem-solving as an ongoing activity.

You will notice that I frequently recommend offsite meetings. Having called many as an executive and having planned and facilitated hundreds as a consultant, I am a strong believer in getting the right people together in a room and guiding them through a process to understand the current reality of the business and its environment, create a clear vision and mission, and build an action plan to get there.

Numerous times in the first months of building an executive team, individual direct reports will raise an issue with you. Whenever the issue involves other members of the executive team, or the effectiveness of the business, ask the person to raise the issue at the next team meeting. It can take three to six months before all the team members begin bringing issues directly to the team meeting without first raising them with you. <u>If you are serious about building a team, you must consistently require people to raise their issues and solve them in the team.</u>

Establishing and Communicating Direction

Establishing, communicating, and sustaining a clear direction for the company are ongoing challenges. People need to work through a process that enables them to develop a depth of understanding of the business and its ever-changing environment.

Periodically, interview your direct reports as part of your leadership practice. Ask each of them to define the company's vision, mission, and strategy. Ask staff at all levels where they think the company is going and if there is anything that they need to do their jobs more effectively. From these conversations, you will learn whether there is a sense of a sharply defined direction among your direct reports and the rest of the company.

At an offsite meeting, have a skilled facilitator take the executive team through a process of developing a common vision, defining a mission statement, and creating, or updating, an integrated strategic plan for the business. The strategic plan may take a series of offsite meetings to complete. In each meeting, key action items will be developed to support the strategy. A member of the executive team should take ownership of each action item.

Following the offsite meetings, work with the team to develop a clear presentation describing the company's strategy and goals. Personally, deliver the presentation to employees at meetings. Ask your direct reports to sit down with the people in their areas of responsibility, review the presentation, engage them in dialogue about it and provide you with a written summary of their issues, concerns, and suggestions.

As you move around the company, engage people in conversations about the company's direction and the key challenges it is facing. Whenever you discover that people are not clear about where the company is going or what its priorities are, <u>tirelessly explain</u> these issues and ask people for their opinions and ideas. Ask your direct reports to follow the same practice when they are with company employees. It will take about six to nine months for you to be able to go into any part of the company and find that people clearly understand the company's direction, challenges, and priorities.

When things change, as they certainly will, redo the process described above. In today's fast-paced world, people are so over-stimulated with information that it requires continual attention to keep an organization focused and executing in the appropriate direction.

Aligning People with the Direction

Once your company's direction has been established and you are sure it is well understood throughout the company, it is time to focus on getting people aligned with it.

You can use several processes to accomplish this. First, take the management team offsite again. This time focus on ways to get people aligned and committed to the business direction. Engage the management team in designing an appropriate program to improve your organization.

Second, follow the offsite meeting with the implementation of the organizational improvement process. Establish functional and cross-functional teams to identify ways of implementing your business plan, identify obstacles and actions to overcome them, and improve work processes.

As you move around the company, engage people in conversations about their work and how it contributes to your company's success. Influence your direct reports to engage in the same types of conversations with their teams. Whenever a significant action is implemented, have the management team explain to employees how it is tied to the company's direction and business plan.

Third, get out into the company and meet personally with staff members in large meetings and small groups to focus on your company's direction and progress. Involve the members of your management team in the group sessions by assigning responsibility to each of them for planning and facilitating meetings.

Finally, pull together small, cross-functional groups for informal conversations over lunch. These kinds of engagements get people involved with and committed to the company's direction and business plan.

Developing Managers and Leaders

Developing managers and leaders is an issue you must take seriously. Again, if you don't, few others will. Make leadership development a key personal responsibility for you and the other members of the executive team.

If you want to have a high-performance company, demonstrate your commitment by insisting that your company have an effective management and leadership development process. Devote at least one offsite per year to reviewing your management and leadership talent and development plans.

As part of the leadership development process, and in preparation for your leadership development review offsite, meet personally with the managers and professionals who report to your direct reports. Ask your direct reports to come to the offsite prepared to discuss the management and leadership capabilities of each of their direct reports and of the people at the next level who work for their direct reports. Expressly require each of your executives to meet one-on-one with the people who work two levels below them.

At your leadership development offsite, walk the executive team through a thorough review of the management and leadership capabilities of the key managers and professionals in the company and review the development plans for each of them.

Following the offsite, take personal responsibility for following the development plans of the people who work for your direct reports. Require the other members of your executive team to take the same responsibility with respect to the development of the people who work for their direct reports. This skip-level responsibility for development is one of the most effective ways I have found to drive effective management and leadership development.

Make management and leadership development a standing issue on the executive team's weekly agenda. Use a portion of the meeting to identify opportunities to give managers and professionals challenging assignments to assess and develop their capabilities.

When an issue needs to be resolved, solicit the names of those who would gain the most developmental benefit from working on the issue. Where practical, assign a team leader and a team to work on the issue. Each time an issue is handled in this way, assign one of the members of the executive team to be an "issue owner" and take responsibility for supporting the team and its leader.

Demonstrate your commitment to development with your executives. Know the capabilities and interests of the members of your team. Look for opportunities to stretch and develop them by delegating tasks and issues that you might otherwise handle yourself.

Most of your key people will have depth in their field or function. Look for opportunities to build breadth of experience by giving them responsibility for things where they have had little or no prior experience. For example, if you have a key management vacancy, give one of your direct report's temporary responsibility for the area while you are recruiting to fill the vacancy. Or, rotate the person into the open position for a period of time and let one of his or her key people take over for him or her.

Another effective developmental tool is to ask your direct reports to delegate key tasks they would normally do themselves to high potential people. The executive can then serve as mentor and coach to the person doing the work.

Month three at GI. We were diligently working on the business agenda we had established for the company when the head of a key function left to take a promotion in another company. Through conversations with my team members, one had indicated he would like to move into general management in the future. He had no experience in this area, but after consultation and thought about the opening on my team, I offered him the opportunity to take on this responsibility. He did and subsequently did a great job at it.

Empowering, Supporting, and Motivating People

Each day brings the opportunity to invest your time and energy in people. Whenever a problem needs to be solved, ask the people closest to the problem to get involved. Create teams made up of executives, managers, and staff members to work together on issues and problems. Ask the teams to develop recommendations and action plans and empower the team to implement them.

If a team's recommendation does not work, or falls short of its objectives, call a meeting to critique the solution. Start by recognizing and rewarding the team for acting. Explain that the critique is to facilitate learning and improvement in the future. Ask questions to probe the team members about what they have learned from their attempt to solve the problem and what they would do differently.

Encourage your direct reports to involve the appropriate people in decision-making and to accept their peoples' decisions whenever possible. Ask them to facilitate learning from decisions that did not work as planned.

When your management team is reviewing progress on an initiative, ask the people actually working on the project to come in to give a briefing and answer questions. Hold critique sessions after major events. Schedule time at key meetings so the staff present at the event can critique the meeting and identify ideas to improve the next event.

In addition to creating an environment in which people are highly involved, find ways to support people on an individual basis. As you move through the company, notice the working conditions: the physical environment your people are working in and the equipment they have to do their work. If you find instances where a person's productivity is being hampered, take their managers aside and ask them why they are not doing something about it. It is surprising what small things, like painting a dingy workspace or replacing an antiquated computer, can mean to people. It says much louder than words that you and the company care about people.

Search continually for accomplishments that are worthy of recognition. Meet frequently with teams and individuals to express your appreciation for how their personal efforts and accomplishments are leading to your company's success.

Establish a recognition system for key projects and activities. Tie personal recognition, time off, small cash bonuses and stock bonuses to the accomplishment of key milestones. Encourage your direct reports to stay alert for performance and effort worthy of recognition and to provide appropriate recognition and rewards for individuals and teams.

Take the time to send a personal email or a handwritten note of appreciation to employees who have made noteworthy contributions to your company.

Identifying and Making Tough Decisions

In your leadership role, be on the lookout for problems and issues that require decisions to move your company forward. Others will make the easy decisions in the everyday course of business. The tough decisions will most often be left for someone else. That's right, you!

You will know you have a tough decision when you find an issue that no one else will do anything about. Most frequently, tough decisions don't get made because there is a lack of consensus in the management team and/or the tough decision will adversely affect one or more key people.

I have experienced many situations in which tough decisions have been left to slide. Unprofitable products, initiatives seriously behind schedule, under-performing executives, unprofitable customers, under-performing business units, and unclear priorities are just a few of the tough decisions I have run into.

Eventually, if not addressed, the tough decisions accumulate to a point where they can threaten the health of the business. Some examples of situations involving tough decisions may be helpful.

Example 1: Product/Service Strategy. Take an issue like product strategy. It is quite common that members of the management team will have committed considerable effort to particular products and services that are or could be sold.

You may find that your company is pursuing multiple product or service initiatives. In many cases, each initiative will have one, or more, management team member(s) who are heavily invested in the success of the initiative. In these situations, it is not uncommon to find that resources are spread over so many initiatives that poor progress is being made on all of them.

In this situation, you must take the lead in analyzing your company's market opportunities and product/service strategy. Would focusing on fewer initiatives and driving them to completion better serve your company?

Take your team through a thorough discussion on opportunities, the resources required by each initiative, and the priorities for each initiative. If there are too many and they can't agree on which initiatives to kill, then the tough decision will be up to you. It's hard to stand in the face of opposition from some, or all, of your management team and make a tough decision to kill an initiative or discontinue a product. If you can't, or won't, do it, it won't happen.

At GI we were developing a product that had been acquired from another company. I became concerned that we were making a substantial investment in it at a time when the marketing and sales budget for our existing products was insufficient to meet our sales goals. After some contentious conversations in the management team, I decided to put the new product on the shelf and allocate its budget to our existing products.

Example 2: Capability of Direct Reports. A key part of your job is to be sure the right people are in the right places. To do this well, it is necessary to thoroughly assess the capabilities of your direct reports. A way to approach this problem is to start with your business strategy and create an organization and staffing plan to implement it.

Use the organization and staffing plan as a guide to define your expectations for each of the positions reporting directly to you. Then take a hard look at each of the people filling those positions.

- Are any of your direct reports under-performing?

- Are any of your direct reports lacking capabilities that are critical for their success in the position?

Once you have answered the above questions, meet with each of your direct reports to share your expectations and dialogue about any concerns you may have. If you have an under-performing person, make the tough decision to confront the issue by making it clear that the person's performance is <u>unacceptable</u>. Establish a 90-day timeline for this person to improve and work with him/her to define 30-, 60-, and 90-day key objectives to improve performance.

If performance does not reach an acceptable level, make the next tough decision: move the person to another job where they can make a contribution, or let them go.

Example 3: Poor Quality. You have significant quality problems with a product/service. You get the management team together and there is no agreement on an appropriate response to the problems. This is the point where you make the tough decision to cease shipping and/or recall the product, or to stop offering the service until the problems are solved. This decision is particularly tough if it will cause a significant loss of revenue for the current quarter, or year. This decision will also put a lot of pressure on your team to solve the problem.

At GI we had a problem with our lead product. We were getting feedback from the field that our product would fail at startup, and users would have to go through two to three of our products to get one that functioned properly. Fortunately, this was not a safety issue, just an aggravation for our users. However, it was a major customer experience issue.

I got the engineering and production teams together to review the problem. We identified the failure modes and set objectives to cure each of them and we stopped shipping the product until all the problems were solved. We put these objectives on a piece of paper and each member of the team signed it. I hung it in a prominent place in my office. As each problem was solved, we put a very visible checkmark beside it. Several items had the checks crossed out and checked again as the team worked to get the problems solved.

When tough decisions are not found and addressed, they can become a considerable drag on the business. Looking for, finding, and promptly addressing them keeps the business moving.

Keeping Yourself Mentally and Physically Fit to Lead

Leading effectively on a daily basis takes a lot of energy. You need to be physically and mentally available to lead. If you allow yourself to become tired or overly stressed, you will have difficulty staying focused, being purposeful, acting rather than reacting, and setting the positive example required to maintain high performance in your company.

To maintain yourself in the high state of physical and mental fitness required to lead effectively, requires that you:

1. Pay attention to your nutrition. Eat a well-balanced diet and avoid over consumption of alcohol and caffeine.

2. Follow a regular program of aerobic exercise.

3. Pace yourself by actively balancing the demands of leadership with rest, recreation, and family.

4. Seek the support of others. Develop and use your network of colleagues for advice and counsel. Be adept at asking for help with difficult problems.

Your daily behavior and the daily behavior of your executive team is the primary factor that drives the effectiveness and performance of your organization. Focusing your attention on leading effectively will create the conditions required to build a high-performance organization. It will also motivate people to create and sustain a superior customer experience.

Chapter 3:
Superior Customer Experience

The journey to a high-performance organization begins with the CEO and the senior leadership team creating an environment that yields superior results and customer experience. The journey begins and ends with the customer.

When I arrived in San Francisco in 1979 to join the Corporate Staff at Transamerica Corporation, I was walking down Montgomery Street on my first day of work when I saw a large cement truck with the slogan "Find a need and fill it" stenciled on its rotating drum.

So simple yet so profound! I often reflect on this advice when I start working for a new client. It is a simple principle. The success of any business ultimately depends on providing products and services that fill important needs for customers. Yet in my experience, it frequently gets lost in many businesses.

The business of my consulting firm, HRMG, LLC, focuses on consulting with boards and executives and their teams, and conducting leadership seminars and workshops. I have had the good fortune to conduct seminars for executives around the world. I frequently start a seminar by asking the participants the question: "What business are you in?" The answers are the software business, the medical devices business, the biotech business, etc. The answers are almost always stated in terms of the product or service their companies produce. Perhaps one time out of one hundred, an executive will say, "I am in the business of helping my customers do 'X.'"

On the consulting side, the business of the firm seems to fall into two clusters. In the first cluster are companies that have gotten themselves into trouble and are trying to bring themselves back, usually with the help of a new CEO. The second cluster consists of businesses that are successful and trying to take their performance to a higher level. In both cases, we start with the customer. Through interviews, focus groups, and survey questionnaires with a representative sample of customers, we try to develop an accurate picture of the experience the customer is having with our client company and its key competitors.

Customer experience is the perception that customers have of what it is like to do business with an organization. This perception is built up out of the transactions the people in customer organizations have with the company. These interactions include people's direct experiences with the company's products and services; interactions with sales and service representatives; communications interactions through internet, telephone, fax, and email; and, in the case of business customers, visits to the customers from the company's executives and other personnel.

An Example of Customer Experience Gone Bad

One day, I received a telephone call from the CEO of a computer software company. This company provided software and services to large and mid-sized companies. The CEO was concerned that his company was beginning to lose sales and customers to competitors and that its customer service ratings had fallen significantly.

We conducted a customer experience assessment. Our interviews, focus groups, and surveys revealed a startling view of the customer experience with our client's business:

1. The latest release of the product was of poor quality. It did not work properly. It contained many bugs, which required many hours of customer time to isolate and correct. Until it was fixed, it disabled key datacenter functions, which created significant risks for customers.

2. Prior to the current release, our client's software was considered reliable but was difficult to install and run properly

in the customers' complex system environments consisting of many brands of hardware and software.

3. Our client's professional services were inadequate. Many customers said the personnel who came to their sites were not capable of helping them effectively solve problems of installation and operation.

4. Customers reported high turnover in our client's service organization, which resulted in frequent changes in the people servicing their accounts. In many instances, customers felt like they were a training ground for our client's personnel.

5. Customers typically ran our client's applications on nights and weekends. They routinely experienced situations in which they would call in for technical support only to find that the highly experienced personnel required to solve their problem had gone home. Customers were frustrated by having to wait one to several days until the needed help became available.

6. The Chief Information Officers of customers reported that our client's executives infrequently visited them and that when they were visited it was almost always a sales call rather than a sincere attempt to understand and help with the CIOs' issues and concerns.

7. Customer CIOs were considering changing to one of our client's competitors.

What would you do if this was the picture of customer experience with your company?

This bleak picture of customer experience was presented to our client's executive team. They were at first somewhat disheartened and resistant. After we showed them a video edited from the customer focus-groups we'd conducted, the gravity of the situation sunk in and they began to focus on solutions.

Based on our experience with similar situations, which indicated that an effective response to serious problems can create a strong and positive customer experience, we saw the situation as a great opportunity for our client to create a response to the situation that would differentiate them from their competitors.

We worked with our client to design and implement a program to address the situation. The client focused on creating a superior experience for its customers. The program involved the senior leadership of the organization and managers and employees from throughout the company.

We helped our client do the following:

1. Look at all aspects of its business from a customer point of view.

2. Identify opportunities to improve customer experience.

3. Design and implement action programs to improve customer experience.

4. Develop and implement a targeted customer visit program by our client's top executives, which focused on building relationships and understanding the business needs of customers' Chief Information Officers.

Within twelve months of the initiation of the program, the company's products were again selling well, its customers had ceased to think about changing to competitors' products, and its external customer survey score had improved and passed the industry average.

Competing on Customer Experience

The case described above is an illustration of the value of focusing on customer experience as a basis of competition. In my work with hundreds of companies, I have found consistently that looking carefully at the experience of customers results in significant opportunities to differentiate your business from your competitors. If your customer experience is not as good as your competitors, you will eventually lose customers and sales. If you can create a customer experience superior to that of your competitors, you will create a competitive advantage.

One of the first tasks of the leader seeking to build a high-performance organization is to get herself and the senior management team grounded in the customer experiences of their own and their competitors' customers.

In the medical devices business, the customer experience chain is complicated. The buying customer is the physician using the device as part of the treatment protocol for a patient. The ultimate beneficiary of the product is the patient who is treated with your device. The product must deliver an effective treatment for the patient and meet the needs and requirements of the physicians using the product.

At GI, this meant getting our oblation and electro-surgery products to work flawlessly and be ergonomically easy for the physician to use. By being continuously in touch with a panel of physicians using our products and following patient volunteers after treatment, we monitored and fine-tuned our customer experience.

Periodically we would bring in a physician or patient volunteer to talk to company employees about using our products and the impact that the procedures that used our products had on patients. These visits were greatly appreciated by our employees and kept us motivated to meet our high standards for product quality and physician support.

Providing a consistent level of superior customer experience requires an organization driven by a clear strategic focus.

Chapter 4:
Clear Strategic Focus

Where are you taking your business?

This deceptively simple question is at the core of defining and communicating the strategic focus of your company. Surprisingly, a simple, agreed-upon, and current expression of business direction does not exist in many organizations.

When clarity of agreement exists, leaders are aligned with a coherent path forward. In its absence, leaders tend to focus on optimizing their own areas of responsibility rather than the whole business.

A clear strategic focus is present when there is:

- A deep understanding of the business environment and how it is expected to change overtime.

- Clarity and agreement among executives and key employees on the current reality and direction of the business.

- A shared sense of ownership for an articulated set of goals and objectives.

- A business agenda that is challenging, yet realistic enough that early successes develop a sense of momentum.

- A set of specified actions and corresponding measurements that enhance business effectiveness and performance in the short run and position the business for continued success.

- An ongoing process of assessing results and adjusting to changes in the business and its environment.

I have conducted hundreds of strategy working sessions to assist management teams to achieve strategic focus. The starting point for any attempt to define strategy is a shared understanding of the current reality. This begins with you thinking through your perceptions of the key aspects of the business.

Once you have clarified your thinking, it is time to systematically enlarge the circle to include all members of the management team. This could take several steps, as it is common for leaders to pull one or two executives into the process before engaging the entire team.

With the advice of the full team, the next step is to engage the business's leadership at several levels in a series of dialogues. These dialogues promote involvement, readiness, and commitment to address the elements required for strategic focus so they can reach deeply into the organization.

The elements of strategic focus are expressed graphically in Figure 1.

Figure 1. The Building Blocks of Strategic Focus

Understanding the Relevant Business Environment

In chapter 1, I shared my first experience with a company trying to adapt to a changing business environment.

In another experience early in my career, I was working for SCM Corporation on the corporate staff. One of SCM's biggest and most profitable divisions, with more than 6,000 employees, was the Typewriter Division headquartered in Ithaca, New York. (There was a time when many students going off to college were accompanied by an SCM portable typewriter).

One day in 1978, I found myself sitting in the office of the division president. We were talking about the strategy for the business when I asked, "So Ernie, what impact are these computerized word processers going to have on your business?"

Annoyed at my impertinence, the division president stood up, pounded his fist on the desk and replied: "People will always need typewriters!" By the time I got back to headquarters in Manhattan, I was sure it was time for me to find another company with which to continue my career (that chance came in the fall of the same year when I was recruited away by Transamerica Corporation).

The division president's lack of openness to consider a fundamental change that was just becoming perceptible in the division's business environment was one of the factors that subsequently led to SCM's demise.

Understanding the business environment is a task that requires continued vigilance and openness to information. For years, the US auto manufacturers ignored the Japanese, who attacked them from the bottom of the product line up into the big cars and trucks. Retailers such as Sears and Penney were slow to react to the threat of online retailers like Amazon.

Building and maintaining a rich understanding of your business environment is essential to maintaining the strategic focus and health of your business. Having a clear and explicit description of what you believe about your business's environment and how it will change over time allows you to scan and monitor it for early warnings of trends that may impact the business. It also provides a context for assessing the current reality of your company.

The Current Reality

SV SHADOWSIDE SHIP'S LOG
JULY 19, 2016243 HRS
LAT: 28° 41.58' N
LON: 142° 39.96' W

On August 28, 2016, my crew and I sailed the *Shadowside* into port in Port Townsend, Washington, after a 4,730 nautical mile voyage from San Francisco to Hawaii and then on to Washington.[10]

Implementing a business strategy is much like navigating a ship at sea. To reach your destination (strategic vision) requires an accurate assessment of your current position (current reality of the business).

Getting a fix on the current reality of a business is often challenging. It requires you and your team to look objectively at your business and rigorously assess each of its major components with respect to their strengths and weaknesses.

It is easy to talk about the things that are going well. People are often reticent to shine a searchlight on the aspects of the business that are not working well or not working at all.

---

[10] The citation from the ship's log above puts the sailing vessel *Shadowside* 1113 nautical miles away from San Francisco in the Pacific Ocean on the way to Kaneohe Bay, Hawaii (see SV-Shadowside.com).

One very helpful process is to put yourself in the position of the beginner. Adopt a point of view that you are the new leader coming to your company for the first time. Here is Alan Mulally's assessment of the Ford Motor Company when he came to the company as CEO in 2006 as given in an interview with Charlie Rose:

Ford had really become a house of brands, as you know. Ford as we know cars, trucks, mustangs. They also have purchased Aston Martin and Jaguar and Land Rover and Volvo. They had taken a 33 [%] equity position in Mazda, and of course they had Ford, Lincoln and Mercury. So really, they were a house of brands now and they had kind of lost what does a Ford brand really stand for. So that was one thing.

So, the next point is they had become very regionalized. So, we had a great Ford of Europe, Ford of the United States, South America, Ford of India, Ford of China. But Henry Ford set Ford up that way because he wanted to participate in the economies, not only provide people with great cars and trucks but also be part of the fabric of the economy in every place of which we operate. But he never anticipated they would operate completely independently. So, there was no synergy and ye[t] we were competing with the best global car companies in the world.

Another really important thing I found was that because of our cost structure and the agreements we had made with UAW; we could not make car[s] in the United States. That's why we were focusing on SUVs and trucks. And if you wanted an Explorer, the best pickup F150, you came Ford. But we weren't making cars anymore.

So, another thing I found was that we were losing money on all the brands and on all the models. And my first forecast that I shared in 2006 was a $17 billion loss for the year for

2006. And so clearly, we needed a different plan and we needed to move decisively.[11]

What can't we talk about? This is one of the questions I ask team members when we are preparing to go offsite to work on strategy. It is an interesting test. In healthy teams, people don't have a list of taboo topics. In less healthy teams, there are often several topics that are off-limits.

At the core, I have found it is the sensitivities of the key leader or team members that determine what issues the team will be willing to put on the table for dialogue.

"Let me have it, with the bark on!"[12]

Your challenge is to create an environment where you and the members of your team can be open and candid about what is happening in the business environment and your business. I have seen more damage to businesses from people sugar-coating or avoiding difficult issues by telling the key leader what they think he/she wants to hear than from any other, single source.

One of the best examples of encouraging a management team to tell it "with the bark on" is given by Alan Mulally in his interview with Charlie Rose:

> **All the leaders are there, the business unit leaders, engineering and manufacturing. We've got about 250 charts we are going through. Everyone shows the plan. Everyone's has the forecast. Everyone is looking for special attention. And, they're all color coded, yellow, green, and red, about how the launch [of the strategy] is going. How**

---

[11] Alan Mulally, CEO of Ford Motor Company interviewed by Charlie Rose 07/27/2011 (https://charlierose.com/videos/15706).

[12] General Pritchard (Millard Mitchell) to Frank Savage (Gregory Peck) when asking him about the failure of one of the Bomb Groups under his command in the movie *Twelve O'Clock High*.

the status is going, how the marketing's going, how the technology's going. And we're doing this for three weeks into it, they have a new [CEO, and, all the charts are green. And, the company was losing 17 billion dollars.] And so, I stopped the meeting, and as nice as I could I said, "Team, is there anything that's not going well?" And of course, the eye contact goes down to the floor.[13]

My advice is to model your willingness to call out the difficult issues in your own behavior and to encourage your team members both verbally and nonverbally to do the same. Sometimes it can take a lot of encouragement to get the level of candor required.

Once you have a good picture of the business environment and the current reality of your business, you can turn your attention to creating a vision to set the destination you are trying to reach.

Vision

I believe that this nation should commit itself to achieving the goal, before this decade is out, of landing a man on the Moon and returning him safely to the Earth. No single space project...will be more exciting, or more impressive to mankind, or more important...and none will be so difficult or expensive to accomplish...[14]

If this initiative is successful, we will have fresh baked products in shops throughout Taiwan within five years.[15]

---

[13] Alan Mulally, CEO of Ford Motor Company interviewed by Charlie Rose 07/27/2011 (https://charlierose.com/videos/15706).

[14] US President John F. Kennedy in a speech to Congress delivered May 25, 1961.

[15] Alfred Chen, Chairman of Namchow Group in a conversation with the author.

The statements above are clear, strategic vision statements. One is for the monumental vision of landing a man on the moon and returning him safely to earth. The other is for a business initiative for my client's firm.

This is the first question for any voyage: Where are we going? And to paraphrase Lewis Carroll:

> **If you don't know where you are going, any route (road) will get you there.**[16]

A business vision establishes a clear picture of where you want your business to be at the end of an increment of time.

For a complex business, the vision can be multifaceted. What markets will we be in? What products/services will we offer? What customers will we target? Where will we be located? What will be our revenues and profits? Where will we be positioned in our industry(ies)?

The answers to these questions define the desired future state of the business and set the stage for defining the mission.

Mission

A business mission is a brief and clear definition of the challenge posed to your company's leadership by your vision. In the two examples given above, there is a straightforward conversion of the vision into a mission statement:

- Land a man on the moon and safely return him to earth by the end of the decade.
- Enable any shopkeeper in Taiwan to make and sell good, fresh-baked products in their shop within five years.
- Become the recognized leader in ease of use and lowest total cost of leasing within three years.

---

[16] Read more at https://www.brainyquote.com/quotes/lewis_carroll_165865.

A more complex vision may require a more elaborate mission statement. However, it all boils down to clearly defining what we aspire to do by when. The next part is the hard part, figuring out the strategy that will fulfill the mission and lead to realization of the vision.

Strategy

A business strategy is the bridge between the current reality of the business and the vision. It is an integrated plan, which answers five key questions:

- How will the conditions, changes, and trends in the relevant environment impact our organization?

- Where are we taking the organization (vision and mission)?

- What are the key initiatives and actions that must be taken to get there?

- What are the target dates for each of the key initiatives and actions?

- Who is responsible (the owner) for each of the key initiatives and actions?

The first challenge is to define the timespan to be covered by the strategy. Most strategies are multi-year in timespan. The fresh-baked products timeline was set for three years. Five years is often a baseline (Ford in 2006). In the case of something as complicated as landing a man on the moon, the timeframe may be ten years or more. I have had several clients who focused on twenty-five and fifty-year timeframes and one who liked to think out one hundred years.

The next challenge is to identify the key initiatives and actions that will be required to bridge the gap between current reality and vision. Defining and laying-out the key actions is a challenging exercise in judgment. It requires enough specificity to clearly define all the key things that need to be done and at the same time be general enough to be grasped and understood by the people who will execute it.

Since most people can only hold five to nine categories in their consciousness at one time, I have found that breaking a strategy down into this number of key components produces a strategy that can be readily communicated and remembered.

Getting a fix on the strategy sets the stage for building the business agenda.

Business Agenda

The business agenda is an action plan that specifies and integrates the key actions that must be taken over time (normally twelve months) to position the business for the future and move the execution of the strategy forward. This plan:

- Specifies the actions required to run the business in the short term,

- Defines the actions required to position the business and achieve its strategy,

- Establishes target dates for agenda items, and

- Assigns accountability and responsibility for these actions by identifying the "owner" who is responsible for execution.

The Case of TransOcean, Ltd.

Prior to its acquisition by Transamerica Leasing, TransOcean Limited (TOL) was one of the top five companies in shipping-container leasing. I had the good fortune to work with TOL for several years leading up to its acquisition. During that period, the

CEO, Greer Arthur, and his team achieved a clear strategic focus for the company.

A careful assessment of TOL's business environment revealed that there was very little, if any, differentiation among the top five competitors. They provided a commodity product, competed on price, and augmented the container fleets owned by the shipping lines. The demand for leased containers was expected to grow at 4 to 5 percent over the next five to seven years, and there was a growing demand for specialized containers such as tanks. Figure 2 is a summary of the team's analysis of TOL's business environment at the time.

Figure 2. TOL
Relevant Environment
Conditions, Changes and Trends

- Industry will grow 3%-4%/year over next 5-7 years

- Top 4 all compete on price

- Shipping lines all expanding own container fleets

- Emerging need for specialized containers (Tank)

In looking at the current reality of their business, the company was clearly standing at number 5 based on capacity. It was hard to admit, but there were no differences among the top competitors in equipment or service. TOL itself had a number of good people but they were underutilized and there were a number of places where important competence was missing.

The team's assessment of TOL's current reality is summarized in Figure 3.

Figure 3. TOL
Current Reality

- #5 in Industry
- No difference
- Good people but underutilized
- Important competence missing (Technical, Quality, Human Resources, Information Systems)

Looking into the future, it was clear to the team that there were clear advantages from scale from both lower financing and operating costs. To continue to succeed it was desirable to move up in industry position. Given its resources and market opportunity, the team believed that TOL could move into the number 3 position through organic growth. Also, at this size, business practices and processes could be streamlined, and it was possible to achieve the lowest total cost of leasing among the major competitors.

In assessing the business from a customer point of view, it became obvious that the process of leasing containers, physically taking control of them, turning them in at the end of a lease and the subsequent repairs required presented a number of difficulties or hassles for customers. This provided an opportunity for differentiation around ease of use.

The TOL vision is summarized in Figure 4.

Figure 4. TOL

Vision

- Move from #5 in industry to #3
- Be the easiest company in the container leasing industry to do business with
- Be the most efficient "lowest total cost"
- Be the #1 choice of customers

To bridge the gap between TOL's current reality and its vision, required a number of strategic initiatives. Improving leadership to bring out the best performance from employees would be a starting point. Improving management of the depots that handled the physical transactions of storing, leasing out, receiving, and repairing containers was a key to reducing hassles and cost as was the improvement of TOL's business processes. Improved container design was targeted to reduce damage and repair cost. Improving information systems to provide real-time transactions by customers would also eliminate hassle and reduce transaction costs. Procuring 150,000 units of container capacity over the next three years would put TOL in the number 3 position. This resulted in the Mission presented in Figure 5 and the Strategy summarized in Figure 6.

Figure 5. TOL
Mission

To become the leader in ease of use and lowest total cost of leasing within three years.

Figure 6. TOL
Strategy

Within three years:

- **Improve leadership capabilities:**
  - **Executive**
  - **Unit & Team**
- **Improve depot management**
- **Improve key business processes**
- **Expand container fleet by 150,000 units**
- **Improve container design to eliminate damage**
- **Use information technology to enable customers to transact business in real time**

The business agenda for TOL focused on four key areas: financial, customers, business processes, and organizational improvement.

The strategy portion of TOL's business agenda is summarized in Figure 7.

Figure 7. TOL
Business Agenda (12 Months)

Customer	• Improve customer experience in all contacts • Implement real time customer transactions • Improve container design	Process	• Redesign business processes: billing, depot management, container leasing, sales • Implement total cost tracking system
Financial	•Acquire 75K container units • Arrange financing for new containers and business improvements • Identify and implement cost savings to maintain profitability	Organization Improvement	• Hire VP Information Systems & VP Technical • Identify and hire people with key capabilities in IS, Technical, Sales • Executives and managers attend: Leading for High Performance and Business Improvement • Implement sales training

Once the strategic focus is clearly established, the next challenge is to structure the organization to run the business effectively and execute the strategy. The starting point for strategy execution is to take a hard look at the organization's structure.

Chapter 5:
The Right Structure

When I first started Covering Ford Motor Company for the *Detroit News* in 2005, the automaker was fighting for its life. I had no idea whether Ford would win or lose, but I knew it would be a great story either way—the end of an American icon, or its salvation.[17]

As with the skeleton that defines the human body, structure defines and limits the functioning of your organization. For instance, Ford Motor Corporation had a dominant, geographical structure, which had evolved to design and produce vehicles for regional/local markets. For a time, this structure worked well.

Then globalization happened. Ford found itself competing with global competitors who were designing and producing cars for global markets that could easily be tailored for regional/local tastes. By 2005 the economies of scale realized by design and production of different models utilizing a single platform put Ford at a sizable competitive disadvantage. No matter what Ford's board and executives tried to do, the company could not overcome the limits of its structure. By 2006 Ford was staring at a loss of 12.6 billion dollars.

The structure of roles and relationships is a key component that contributes to the effectiveness of every organization. The right structure of clearly defined roles, responsibilities, relationships, and levels supports mutual trust, effective performance and collaboration

---

[17] Hoffman, Bryce G. *American Icon: Alan Mulally and the Fight to Save Ford Motor Company*. New York: Currency Books, 2012, p. ix.

across levels and functions. The wrong structure produces mistrust, conflicts, confusion, and diminished performance.

Differentiation and Integration

Organizations grow through a process of repeated cycles of differentiation and integration. Things start simply enough. A few people get together around an idea for a product or service. They write a business plan and raise some money. They design and build the first generation of a product or create a service and go looking for customers. If they are successful, they find a market for their offering and begin to acquire more customers.

Soon they need customer service, marketing, accounting, production/operations, sales, product, human resources, and engineering functions and the people to staff them. The company is now differentiated and faces the challenges of getting the parts to align and work together effectively. Business plans, processes, policies and procedures are developed and implemented to align and integrate peoples' efforts.

More success brings more people and layers of management begin to appear. Markets expand, necessitating organizational components in different geographies. More markets, more customers, more products and services and before long a global business emerges. A company like Amazon goes from a garage startup to a global company of 647,000[18] employees in a period of twenty-four years.

Getting the structure right is a continuing challenge. As your business grows and changes, the structure evolves. Changes in structure are made to accommodate differences in personal capability, and markets. Layers are added to facilitate the

---

[18] McCracken, Harry. https://www.fastcompany.com/90331689/amazons-wild-24-year-ride-from-11-employees-to-600000-plus, April 11, 2019.

management of people and resources. Many Band-Aids may be applied to adjust to specific problems and situations. Over time, it is natural for the organization to evolve in ways that detract from overall effectiveness and efficiency.

Roles

What you want from your structure is to focus activity, responsibility, and accountability. Let's start with role of the chief executive officer (CEO).

The CEO Role

Whether you are the CEO of a small, early stage company or a global behemoth like Ford, you are unique in that you are the one person who has responsibility and accountability for the whole enchilada. You are responsible and accountable for the strategic health of the organization.[19]

What's important to the strategic health of the business?

This is the fundamental question that guides me when I sit down with a CEO to talk about structure. My basic rule of organization is that if it is critically important to the strategic health of the company, it is a key executive role and should report to the CEO.

Key Executive Roles

For example, one of my clients was running a company that had grown quite large around a mature, core business. Key among his

---

[19] Strategic health is an organizational state in which short- and long-term goals, objectives, and actions are balanced; and adaptability, innovation, continuous learning and improvement, and speed are pursued as paths to superior results. It is the process of attracting, energizing, focusing, aligning, and retaining people to accomplish results and build a highly effective organization.

strategic concerns was the need to grow the company into other lines of business. The company had tried for several years to develop new lines of business with little success. Despite putting very good people in charge of these efforts, little progress was made. On examination, it turned out that all of the new business efforts were done as part of the mature business.

I had first encountered this situation when I joined the corporate staff at Transamerica Corporation. At that time, Transamerica was a diverse multi-market company. In addition to a large group of insurance and financial service businesses, it had a portfolio of operating companies including Delaval (industrial products), Budget Rent-a-Car, United Artists Corporation (motion pictures), Transamerica Relocation Services and Transamerica Leasing (shipping containers).

One of the things I learned at Transamerica was that each of these businesses had to be competitive in its relevant business environment. Each needed to invest to maintain and enhance its competitive and market position. This was something that was made difficult by the role of the headquarters in allocating investment among the subsidiary companies. Also, each of these businesses had idiosyncrasies. The compensation of the CEO of United Artists was much greater and his company car much grander than that of the CEO at Delaval, or the CEO of Transamerica itself.

The situation with my client was not surprising to me, as I have encountered this situation numerous times. A large, mature business focuses on effectiveness, efficiency, and cost control. It necessarily needs to be tightly run. A new, early stage business needs to have freedom to innovate. It needs to experiment to learn its way to success in its market. It needs to emphasize effectiveness over efficiency.

For my client, the solution was to structure the company to run both the mature business and the new businesses. This was accomplished by having two Executive Vice Presidents, one for the mature business and one for new businesses. Each new business was then organized as an independent business unit under the new business EVP.

This also occurs with other functions. Are people and talent critical to your business? If so, does the head of human resources report directly to you? What about product development? The first step in getting your structure right is to take the people out of it and take a hard look at your current business and your strategy. What structure will provide the right focus, responsibility, and accountability to run the current business effectively and implement the strategy?

Once you get the key executive line structured properly, you can determine if you have the right people to staff it (see chapter 6).

Levels[20]

The next step is to have each of your key executives answer the question of what structure is critical for them to execute their responsibilities. Again, take the people out. Then, get this level staffed with the right people and repeat the process until you get down to the first level of individual contributors.

By this point you will have a hierarchical structure of several levels. In implementing or revamping an organization's structure, it is necessary to confront the issue of how many levels is right at this point in the company's evolution. The goal is to have the right number of levels for the size and complexity of the organization. Too few or too many levels will impair effectiveness and efficiency.

---

[20] In working with the challenges of organization structure, I have found the work of Elliott Jaques to be highly useful. Elliott Jaques, *Requisite Organization* (Arlington, VA: CASON Hall, 1998) and Elliott Jaques, *Social Power and the CEO: Leadership and Trust in a Sustainable Free Enterprise System* (Westport, CT: Quorum Books, 2002).

Answering this challenge requires an understanding of the nature of work and the size of jobs.

A company (government agency or the administrative function of a charity) is an organization designed to get things done to accomplish a purpose. In thinking about structure, it is helpful to start with the basic nature of work and work roles.

Work

Work consists of one or more persons using discretion to solve problems to accomplish an objective (what) by a target completion time (when) within prescribed limits (legal, ethical, policy, and practice). In short, a unit of work is a "what by when to be accomplished within limits."

Work Roles (Jobs)

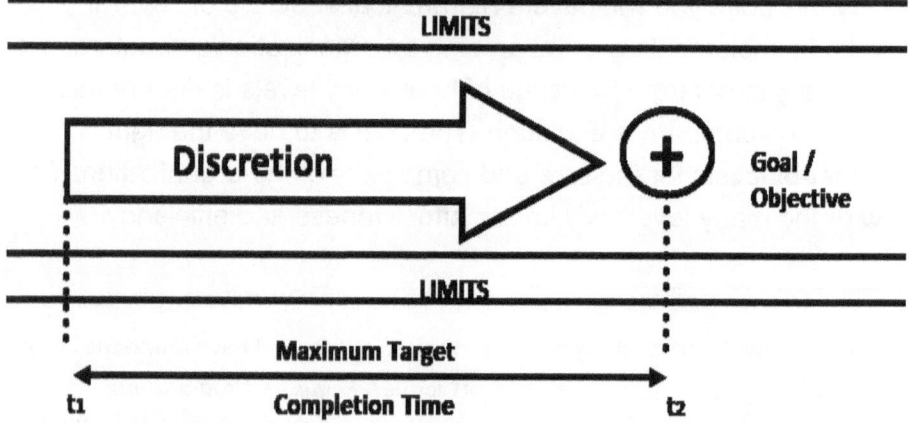

Figure 8.
JOBS: DEFINITION OF WORK
Work = Exercise of discretion within limits to achieve an objective within maximum target completion time.

A work role (job) can be thought of as a playing field (Figure 1.) The targeted completion time establishes the length of the field. The limits establish the width. The person occupying the role plays by using their discretion to apply knowledge, skills and judgement to overcome obstacles and achieve the objectives.

A work role is a grouping of work that is designed to be delegated to a person who is expected to use appropriate discretion and to be held accountable for completing it. Work roles are the most basic of organizational components. Similar work roles are grouped into units, units into functions, functions into larger organizations.

For the purpose of designing an organization structure, it is useful to consider how big roles (jobs) are at each level. There are many approaches to this challenge. The one I have found most useful is to focus on the *time-span of discretion*. The time-span of a role is defined by the longest targeted completion time required to accomplish the objectives of the role.[21]

A small role has objectives with short target times and tight limits. A large role has objectives with long target times and wide limits. Illustrative organization levels, roles and time-spans are presented in Table 1.

[21] Elliott Jaques, *Requisite Organization*. (Arlington, VA: CASON Hall, 1998), 37-39.

Table 1. Organizational Level – Time Span - Role		
Level	**Time Span**	**Role**
VIII	50Y+	Chairman, CEO (Very Large, Global Company Amazon, Ford, Google, US President)
VII	20Y-50Y	CEO or COO
VI	10Y-20Y	EVP or SVP - Line or Headquarters Staff Head Business Unit President
V	5Y-10Y	Senior Staff CEO or Business Unit President
IV	2Y-5Y	Unit Manager Functional Head
III	1Y-2Y	Unit Manager Staff Specialist
II	3M-1Y	First Line Manager Staff Specialist
I	1D-3M	Operating Employees

Source: Elliott Jaques, *Requisite Organization* (Arlington Virginia: CASON Hall, 1998), 41.

Time-span is the longest time into the future that the role requires planning and execution to achieve the objective. It provides an objective measure of the complexity of the role. The guiding principle is that each level of organization should allow the incumbents to do work that is different (more complex) than their direct reports.

If the complexities of a manager's and subordinate's roles are too close or the same, they will tend to get in each other's way. One or both of them will be frustrated. If there is a large gap between the complexities of the manager's and subordinate's roles, the manager will most likely be frustrated that he or she is being dragged down into too much detail, and the subordinate will most likely be frustrated that he or she is getting too little direction from the manager.

Using time-span as a guide (Table 1.), the maximum levels you would want in a large, global organization would be eight from top to bottom. For a global, midsized growth company, you would have seven. For a mature, early stage company, you would have five levels.

Using the time-span of roles to level the organization structure also sets the stage for understanding the level of complexity capability that is required for people to perform the role effectively. I will return to this topic in chapter 6, where we will explore understanding the critical requirements of jobs and assignments and selecting the right people for them.

Chapter 6:
The Right People

It was a Friday morning. I was meeting with Eric, CEO of a global consumer products company. Eric was talking about his key staff:

"Mary is a good communicator. People understand what she is thinking and what she wants from them. But, they do not like working for her because she is judgmental and very critical of them."

"Logan is full of energy and very smart. When he has an assignment, he jumps into it right away with great enthusiasm. After about forty-five days, things are a mess. He always neglects the organizing, planning, and collaboration required to lead a project to full and effective execution. Initiatives he leads rarely achieve the desired results and most often come in well behind schedule and over budget."

"Rob. Everyone wants to work for Rob. People like him. He is fair. He is also warm and personable. His difficulty is communication. People have a hard time understanding what he is thinking about key issues and what he expects them to do."

The following Tuesday, I was with Barbara, CEO of a business services company. She was talking about her vice president for national accounts:

"There has been no change with him. Despite my coaching and cajoling, he continues to call on only those accounts where he has friends. His performance in new accounts, which are 70 percent of his incentive bonus, is miserable."

A few days later, I was meeting with Kirk, Chief Operating Officer of a large software company. He was concerned about leadership:

> **"Our senior management team is good enough. What we lack is bench strength. We just don't have enough strong leaders at the director and manager levels."**

These comments are typical of the conversations that I have been having with senior executives for more than forty years. People issues are one of the most frequent and critical concerns of the executives with whom I have worked. These are the issues that come up most frequently:

- The challenge of thinking systematically about the people in a complex organization.

- Deciding who the "right" people are for the organization.

- Understanding the critical requirements of jobs and assignments.

- Assessing the people in key assignments.

- Selecting the right people for jobs and assignments.

- Developing people for key leadership positions.

- Handling performance problems.

- Facing up to tough decisions about the "wrong" people.

Getting the right people into the right jobs is critical to creating a high-performance organization. It is one of the key challenges for you and your executive team.

Thinking about Your Organization's People

When it comes to the quality of an organization's people, I find it helpful to think about people in four groups:

1. The members of the executive team.

2. The leadership network, which is composed of the key managers and key technical people who are critical to the success of the business.

3. The solid employees and managers who do the day-to-day work of getting things done.

4. The marginal employees, who are performing below standard.

The Executive Team

The members of the executive team are critical to the process of building a high-performance organization. They are so critical that I believe a business leader needs to have a trusted advisor with whom to talk about the key people on his or her staff.

A highly capable executive team is a necessary ingredient in building a high-performance organization, but it is not sufficient in and of itself. Leadership is required throughout the organization from a network of managers and individual contributors.

The Leadership Network

Every organization has (or should have) a core of highly capable managers and individual contributors who provide leadership to the rest of the organization on a daily basis. High-performance organizations have a critical mass of talented people in this group and they are linked together into an effective network.

Building an effective leadership network takes an investment of time and resources. It requires the executive team to identify the leaders in the organization at all levels.

A process must also be designed and implemented to bring these people together so they can get to know each other. Leadership development workshops and offsite meetings focusing on the strategic and operational plans of the business are an excellent way to build a leadership network. Calling upon members of the leadership network to serve on task forces and teams to solve specific business problems is another way to strengthen the network.

Solid Citizens

Although leaders are important, the number of them is generally much smaller than the total number of employees, supervisors, and managers. It is easy to overlook the contribution of those people who come to work every day and put in a good day's effort on the company's behalf. These "solid citizens" are the life's blood of any organization. Their well-being needs to be a key focus of all the company's leaders.

It seems trite to say that a substantial amount of leadership time needs to be invested in acknowledging and appreciating the solid citizens in your company. However, I find that in many of the organizations with which I have worked, these people are taken for granted.

In the best companies I have experienced, the leadership spends a significant amount of time walking around and engaging employees in dialogue and appreciating their efforts. These companies also focus on maintaining and enhancing the competence and capabilities of their solid citizens through appropriate training and development.

Your efforts and those of the executive team in this area are critical. It is natural and easy to focus on star performers and high potentials. However, it is the solid citizens that keep the business running from day-to-day and provide the platform for the stars and high potentials to shine. We all know the star quarterbacks of our favorite football teams. How many of their offensive line can you name?

Marginal Employees

At any given time in most companies, there are a few employees performing below standard. This situation may be the result of jobs or assignments changing to a higher level of complexity (fit), hiring or promotion errors, employees losing interest in their jobs, or other issues such as sickness.

Tolerance of non-performers is one of the surest ways to injure the motivation and performance of good employees. People quickly become frustrated and angered when other employees are allowed to under-perform with no consequences.

I have observed the impact of allowing non-performance and under-performance on the factory floor, among professional contributors and middle managers, and in executive teams.

This is an area where it is critical to have an effective process for setting performance standards and objectives and assessing peoples' performance on an ongoing basis. A good performance management process is not sufficient, however. Managers and leaders must have the will to address performance problems as they arise. Situations of under-performance must be confronted, analyzed to determine the root causes, and resolved.

One of my clients, Phil Kantz, the CEO of a global equipment leasing company, had a good approach to the problem of non-performers. The standard he set for the company was "get good or get gone." By this, he meant that every person was expected to perform his or her job well. He held the company's managers to a 90-day standard to resolve performance problems once they were identified.

In cases where non-performance was due to a poor fit between the person and his or her job, every effort was made to match the person to a job in which they could contribute to the company at an acceptable level of performance. If an employee was unable or unwilling to perform at an acceptable level in his or her job, they were severed from the company.

Good People and Good Fit

I was talking about the challenge of staffing for high performance one day with my client, Greer Arthur, who had founded and built his business into a high-performance company over a period of twenty-five years. His answer was:

"Get good people."

What Greer meant by "good people" was that they:

1. Are strong on the basics of honesty and integrity.

2. Are highly motivated to perform well.

3. Seek to continuously learn and develop their capabilities.

4. Possess potential to grow into more responsible positions and roles.

5. Play well as team members.

6. Possess the competencies required to perform at a high level in the jobs and roles they are in or are being selected for.

There is a problem in the above list, however. The list combines two ideas, the attributes of a good person and the idea of a good fit.

Item number six in the list above is the really critical one. A person can be a "good person" who possesses all the other qualities in the list and not be a "good fit" if they do not have the knowledge, skill, and experience to perform at a high level in their specific role or assignment.

So, I would adapt Greer's advice this way:

Get good people who are good fits.

Getting the "right people" means getting people who are both good persons and good fits by assuring that, in addition to meeting items 1–5, they are a good match for the job, role, or assignment they are in or going to be in. Getting the right people involves practicing hiring up, avoiding hiring down, and having an effective way to address selection errors.

Hiring Up

This is another key idea for which I must thank Greer. I had observed that he was very active in his company's hiring. He was highly concerned with the quality of the people at his company.

His philosophy was to "hire up," by which he meant that when you have the opportunity to hire someone, hire a person who is better than you. His concern was that in his experience people frequently "hired down." By hiring down, he meant they would hire someone just a bit weaker than they were.

I have observed these processes at work in numerous companies. The companies that focus a great deal of attention on hiring and practice hiring up perform at a higher level than the companies that are lax on hiring and where hiring down tends to become the norm.

It does not take very long for a company to become weak with respect to having the right people if its hiring practices allow, or even encourage, hiring down. In my experience, the only way to stay strong from a "right people" point of view is to assure that the hiring process and practices result in continuous hiring up.

In high-performance companies, the CEO takes a direct and personal interest in the people being hired by his or her direct reports. The CEO also requires members of the executive team to be involved in the hiring by directors and managers. Hiring, like leadership development, profits from the skip level approach.

Handling Selection Errors

No matter how good our selection process and practices, selection errors will occur. Sometimes, it is obvious quite quickly that the wrong person has been selected for a job or assignment. Usually it takes several months, or more, to realize the person is a poor fit.

What is important is to confront the situation as soon as you are aware of it. These are the questions to answer:

- How severe is the lack of fit?

- Is there a realistic path to grow this person into the job?

- How long will it take?

- Is there a way to offset the person's weaknesses while they are growing into the job?

Based on the answers to these questions, it will become clear if there is a way to recover from the selection error, or if it will have to be undone by severing the person from the company.

Acting decisively when a selection error has been recognized is often difficult. My experience has been that there is a pronounced tendency in most organizations to "just give it more time." My observation is that the more time that goes by, the more difficult it is to rectify the situation.

There is usually little to be gained by prolonging the agony of the decision and communication with the person involved. I have found it is better for both the company and the person to recognize the situation and take the steps necessary to either bring the person into a good fit with the job or get them moving along with their career outside the company.

Swift action is required when a key executive is incapable of meeting the requirements of his or her job. When action is not taken, every day that goes by brings more harm to a key part of the organization. Important things do not get done, valuable people may leave the organization, and it becomes difficult to recruit good people to replace them.

Assessing People in Key Assignments

Clear assessment criteria and an effective performance-assessment process are essential to building and sustaining a high-performance executive team and leadership network.

Assessing the Executive Team

We all know the legend of King Arthur and the Knights of the Round Table. One of your key decisions will be choosing who is going to have a seat at your table. When it comes to building and sustaining a high-performance organization, the key executive group that sits at your table is of critical importance.

The first step in assessing your executive team is to define the core criteria required to attain and remain in an executive position in your company. In my view, key executives must meet the following criteria:

1. Possess the intellectual capabilities and business experience necessary to understand the business environment and contribute to the strategy and direction.

2. Have highly effective leadership capabilities to mobilize their people, focus their efforts to execute the business plan, and develop leadership talent.

3. Exhibit high standards of personal integrity and ethical conduct.

4. Possess the technical capabilities to direct their areas of responsibility.

5. Hire and surround themselves with highly capable people.

6. Be capable and willing to work as members of a team.

7. Be willing to enthusiastically put their capabilities to work for the best interests of the organization.

These are the most useful core criteria I have found for making decisions about key executives.

Assessing the Leadership Network

The next step is to assess the quality of this group. Assessing the quality of the leadership group involves taking a close look at their knowledge, skills, and experience in four key areas:

- Functional competence—do they possess the appropriate level of knowledge and experience in their function to perform effectively?

- Business competence—do they have the appropriate level of knowledge and understanding of the business to make effective decisions?

- Management competence—do they have the appropriate management capabilities to plan, organize, and execute as individuals, team members, and managers?

- Leadership competence—do they exhibit the ability and skill to attract, energize, focus and align people to accomplish results?

If the quality of your leadership network is not strong, a program of upgrading through training, development, and replacement will be necessary.

Having an effective assessment process and discipline is a necessary but not sufficient condition for developing and sustaining high performance. Your company must also do the difficult work of confronting and working through performance problems.

Handling Performance Problems

This is another area in which you and the members of your executive team must take leadership and set the example for the rest of the company. My advice is clear. Assess the executive team and members of the leadership network on an ongoing basis. As soon as you are clear that an executive or network member is faltering on any of your assessment criteria, it is time to act.

1. **Confront the problem**. Sit down with the person. Share your perspective on the problem. Ask for their perspective. Listen carefully. Be sure the person knows their job is on the line. (This can be a challenge. The person may not want to hear it. And/or, you may not want to say it clearly and unequivocally.) Set a time to get back together with them to do some problem solving, unless you are in situation (5) below.

2. **Create a plan of action**. If there is a concrete plan to bring the person to an acceptable level of performance in an acceptable period of time, implement it and monitor the results. This may include adding someone to his or her team that has the strengths to offset the person's weaknesses.

3. **Address a lack of fit**. If he or she is a good person in the wrong job (bad fit), and if there is a job or assignment where the person can add real value to the company, offer it to them. However, let it be their choice as to taking the job or leaving the company.

4. **Make the tough decision**. If there is no path to successful performance, or there is no time to implement a plan, remove the person from the job.

5. **Unacceptable behavior**. If it is a matter of integrity or unethical or illegal behavior, remove them from the company immediately.

This is a tall order. I have now worked with over 300 executive teams. Each posed its own challenges. In my own experience as a CEO, I have had the luxury of building two executive teams from scratch and have stepped into situations where the individual executives were in place long before I arrived. As a consultant and business advisor, I have been through situations that range from requiring the replacement of one or two key executives to a critical need to replace most of the team members.

Failure to Perform

The easiest situations are those where it is clear that one or more of the key executives must be replaced because of failure on one or more of the criteria outlined above. In these situations, it is just a matter of doing the difficult work of confronting the issue, severing the executive(s) in question and getting on with the task of replacing them.

The most difficult situation that I have personally faced was when I built a team from scratch. I had an assignment that involved leading a critical technical area. I had a person who had worked for me in a previous company who had done a good job in this area. Like many

CEOs in a new assignment, I reached for someone I had experience with.

It took about six months before it became clear that the job in my new company was far more complex and challenging than the one in my former company. Unfortunately, my person was just not capable of doing the job at this level of complexity and challenge (a bad fit). Coming to the realization that I had to let him go was excruciatingly painful. Despite the fact that I gave him a very good severance package, our relationship was fractured beyond repair.

I have experienced the situation described above a number of times with clients. It usually proves as or more difficult for them as it was for me. It frequently results in an irreparable break in the relationship.

In the worst cases, I have seen otherwise good CEOs drag their feet on this decision for prolonged periods. In several cases, I have seen good CEOs lose their jobs due to their inability to come to terms with the failing performance of people they have brought into the company or worked with for a long time. When the board of directors becomes concerned about this issue, it's too late. The CEO has then lost some credibility and confidence with the board.

My advice is to be especially careful about bringing people you have worked with in other contexts into the organization. Be sure there is a good job/person fit before doing so. There is also the negative impact on the organization of creating an "in group" who all worked together at another company.

Unacceptable Behavior

One of the most difficult situations, which I have encountered numerous times, involves a member of the executive team who uses his or her relationship with the CEO to try to influence and control other members of the team.

At one client, an executive consistently volunteered to take ownership of difficult problems facing the CEO. The CEO in turn grew to appreciate this executive's help. The executive created the perception in the executive team that he had a special relationship with the CEO. He then used this perception to influence and control his colleagues for the benefit of his area of responsibility and himself. It took a long time for the CEO to discover that this executive was giving illegitimate directions to other members of the team in the CEO's name. This breach of integrity should be grounds for immediate dismissal.

Another difficult situation occurs when there are one or more executives on the team who are pretending to go along with the CEO's direction but fighting it behind his or her back. In meetings they are all smiles and nods of agreement. Back in the organization they are critical of the strategy and direction.

In the bad cases, passive resistance turned into active attempts to subvert the strategy and action agenda. In the worst cases, there were undeclared wars between key executives and the CEO that were tearing their organizations apart. This type of situation is another severe breach of integrity requiring immediate action.

Facing Up to Tough Decisions about the "Wrong" People

A high-performance organization treats people with dignity and respect. This includes letting them know where they stand with the company, giving them a chance to adapt to changing conditions, and having appropriate processes for dealing with problems, such as lack of fit and poor performance, and severing people from the company when necessary ("get good or get gone").

This process is complicated by the fact that people are human beings with feelings, hopes, aspirations, dreams, and families who depend on them. This makes it difficult to take timely action to address performance issues and often results in incrementally giving the situation more time to correct itself or just living with it. Situations involving people who have worked for your company for a long time are often very difficult.

If the executive leadership won't step up to these tough situations and decisions, they can go on and on, to the detriment of your organization.

Understanding the Critical Requirements of Jobs and Assignments

Finally, I would have to make a decision on the ground assault element (for the Operation to Kill or Capture Osama bin Laden). Would I choose Navy SEALs or Army special operations? There were only two men I trusted well enough to lead the ground operation. Both officers were extremely experienced in combat, both superb tacticians, and most importantly, I felt, both were consummate team players. With all the tension that would invariably develop as a result of this high-profile mission, I needed someone who could calmly build the joint operational team and not get over pressurized when the stakes got high.[22]

Selecting people to fill key executive positions and assignments is one of the most critical decisions facing board members and senior executives. Key positions and assignments are "high-leverage" roles.

---

[22] McRaven, Admiral William H. *Sea Stories: My Life in Special Operations*. New York: Hachette Book Group, Inc., 2019, p.290.

The performance of the person selected can affect many people inside and outside the organization.

Effective leadership performance maintains and improves your organization's ability to perform. Ineffective performance leads to impairment of your organization's ability to achieve results. Critical customers and employees may be lost, and your competitive position may be severely damaged.

The Case of Andy F.

The case of Andy F. illustrates how a person can appear to be a good candidate when, in fact, he is a poor match to the assignment.[23] Andy F. interviewed well. On paper he was the ideal candidate for Chief Executive Officer of Special Technology, Inc. He had served as the President of his previous employer's largest division for five years. His financial results were the best in the company. He was liked and respected by customers, suppliers, and employees. He was well regarded for his contributions as a member of the firm's senior management committee.

The selection process used by Special Technology was thorough. Candidates were interviewed by the Selection Committee of the Board. Three finalists were then interviewed by the remaining board members and key executives who would report to the new CEO. The Selection Committee gathered feedback from the executives and the full board devoted a significant amount of time to reviewing the candidates and coming to a decision. Andy was selected by the board.

After eighteen months as the CEO of Special Technology, Inc., Andy was failing. The company was in trouble. It lacked direction. There was discord on Andy's management team. Key customers

---

[23] The names have been changed to protect the identities of the people and organization described herein.

were shifting to competitors' products. Financial performance was beginning to trend down and investors were getting nervous. At this point, I was retained by the board to assess the situation.

What Happened?

Andy's case is a prototypical example of how, on paper and in interviews, an executive can meet carefully-thought-out selection criteria and yet fail to produce the successful performance anticipated by his new employers and him/herself. Executive selection errors occur when board members or senior executives fail to understand:

- Behavioral requirements of the job.

- Personal attributes of the chosen executive.

- Conditions under which past performance was achieved.

Behavioral Requirements of the Job

Executive jobs and assignments may appear to be highly similar. They require knowledge of the business and industry; competence in finance, marketing, and operations; the ability to lead people; and the capacity to engage and relate effectively to employees, customers, suppliers, investors, and in some situations the community in which a company is located. But here the similarity ends.

The specific assignment and the conditions surrounding it frequently require unique combinations of competence for success to be achieved. They require a person whose capability to deal with complexity meets or exceeds the complexity (time-span) of the role.

Andy's position provides an example of the uniqueness of executive jobs. Special Technology was a freestanding company.

Andy reported to a board of directors who were not fully aware of the company's current condition.

Special Technology had been coasting for several years while its previous president was preparing to move to a new company. The primary focus of the previous CEO had been on good financial performance. Expenditures on new product development, automation, hiring, and training had been systematically trimmed to keep the bottom line growing despite nearly flat revenues. Several key members of the management team had left to be replaced by less experienced (i.e., less expensive) people. Customers had become concerned about declining service, while competitors were pressing with new products that were challenging Special Technology's product line.

Special Technology required a revitalization to regain its customer focus and some bold programs to restore its competitive leadership. There were several key behavioral requirements of the CEO's job:

- Quickly size up the condition of the business.

- Evaluate the competence of key staff and quickly replace those who did not have the capability to move the company forward.

- Repair strained client relationships and hold them until new products could be brought to market.

- Develop a strategy to focus the company and greatly improve its operations, products, and quality in order to regain its competitive position.

- Clearly communicate the strategy to customers, employees, and investors.

- Execute the strategy and produce visible results.

Attributes of the Candidate

Lacking a capable internal candidate, the board had turned to external sources. Andy was one of several candidates. On paper he was strong. The division he was leading had a good record of both growth and financial performance. He was well-regarded by everyone who knew him.

He impressed the board with his practical approach, visible ease with people, and orientation toward action. In the absence of a detailed knowledge of the condition of Special Technology and a behavioral profile of the CEO's job, the board was unanimous in its endorsement of Andy.

Andy joined the firm and began a flurry of activity. He met with his staff, employees, and customers. He traveled extensively, held meetings, and tried to build consensus on problems and potential solutions. For the first six-to-nine months, things seemed to go well. He got key customers to commit to staying with the company until he could implement changes. He established relationships with people at all levels. He focused enthusiastically on problems and solved them quickly, although many of his initial decisions had to be revisited and changed downstream. These "quick fixes" that proved to be ineffective became a source of frustration for members of his management team.

As Andy entered his second year as CEO, things were beginning to turn down. Each major change that he tried to implement met with resistance from one or more factions on his management team. Without consensus, he found it hard to move forward. As he got to know his key people, he found several of them to be less competent than their jobs required. He found it very difficult to confront them with the shortcomings in their performance. His response was to dig deeply into the details of their operations, to which they reacted with strong but well-hidden resentment.

The company had no direction. Andy seemed to jump from one short-term problem to another. Some of the customers he had retained now became disenchanted with the lack of tangible results and switched to competitors' products. Andy responded by launching a cost-cutting program to save the bottom line.

Andy's behavior was consistent with his personality. His key personal attributes included:

- A strong, outward focus on people.

- A concrete, practical, present-time orientation and the need to focus on the facts and details of any situation or problem.

- A subjective and personal decision-making style that was highly sensitive to the needs of others.

- A need for harmony and consensus.

- A preference for keeping things open and flexible and for responding to problems and opportunities spontaneously as they arose.

- Pronounced needs to personally perform at a high standard of excellence and to take personal responsibility for problems and their solutions.

- A need to be liked and accepted by others and to form close relationships.

- The lack of a well-developed capability to influence others.

Andy's personal attributes were poorly matched with the behavioral demands of the job. Key behavioral demands were beyond his personal capabilities. These demands included developing a strategic plan, objectively evaluating key people, taking action to confront performance problems, replacing people, delegating important tasks and initiatives, holding people accountable, balancing strategic and operational needs of the business, and tightly organizing his personal priorities and time.

How could Andy have been so successful in his previous position and where did the board go wrong?

Conditions Under Which Past Performance Was Achieved

Unquestionably, Andy had achieved great success with his former company. But a close look at the environment in which he had flourished reveals a set of conditions that differed significantly from his position as CEO of Special Technology, Inc.

- **The Complexity of the Job**. The division president's job that Andy came from was significantly less complex than the CEO's job at Special Technology. The CEO's job required the ability to recognize and handle a much more challenging set of behavioral requirements in a less structured and significantly more challenging environment over a longer time-span.

- **Corporate Culture and Management Processes**. In his previous company, Andy reported to a strong group executive who was primarily responsible for the long-term, strategic direction of the businesses that reported to him. There was a formal planning process at the corporate level that was designed to achieve an appropriate balance between short-term operating decisions and long-term strategic direction. Andy's major contribution was to execute in a highly structured environment on a strategy that was largely developed by the Group Executive with Andy's input.

- **Executive Team Capabilities and Teamwork**. Andy's previous management team, composed of highly competent executives, had worked together for several years. The capabilities of the individuals on the team complemented Andy's personality and highly participative style. They left Andy free to do what he did best, which was to relate to employees, customers, suppliers, and corporate senior management.

- **State of the Business**. The former business had been very healthy when Andy became its president. The division's financial performance was sound. It had a reservoir of new products ready to be brought to market. It also had a well-established history of investing in people, products, and technology to continuously improve its market position.

In summary, Andy's previous company provided an environment that allowed Andy to make the most of his personal assets. The level of complexity matched Andy's capability. It also had people and processes that effectively neutralized or offset Andy's personal weaknesses as an executive.

After assessing the situation, I reported to the board that Andy was significantly mismatched to the CEO's job and that the situation, which had been a revitalization, was now a turnaround.

In a rather tense board meeting, I made my report and answered questions. I then asked each board member to share their reaction to the situation and my report. As we went around the table, it became clear that Andy needed to be replaced.

How could this selection error have been avoided?

Selecting the Right People for Jobs and Assignments

The recruitment, selection, and hiring of key executives is time-consuming and costly. It can take from one to three years to know if the hired executive will be effective.

If the executive proves to be ineffective, the process of confronting the problem and completing an outplacement is also time-consuming and costly. The damage to the organization in cost, diminished performance capability, missed market opportunities, and losses in competitive position can be catastrophic. Although the full impact of a key executive selection error is rarely calculated, it is clear these decisions are among the most critical made by board members and senior executives.

The selection error made by the board in Andy's case could have been avoided by using a systematic, job/person matching process. Such a process would have helped the board to understand the behavioral requirements of the CEO's job, Andy's personal attributes, and the conditions under which he was likely to perform well or poorly.

Job/person matching is a systematic process that makes use of behavioral job analysis, behavioral interviewing, and instrumented assessment to profile people and jobs and to determine the degree of match between them. It requires a practitioner who is knowledgeable about high-level executive jobs and has well-developed capabilities in this process.

Behavioral Job Analysis

Information is obtained about the conditions surrounding the job and the key tasks and challenges that must be effectively handled to achieve high performance. This information is gathered through interviews of people who are close to the target job or assignment. These are analyzed to produce a profile of critical behavioral demands that must be met for successful job performance. The profile serves as a template for the assessment of candidates.

Behavioral Interviews and Instrumented Assessment

Behavioral interviews focus on the actual experience of candidates in meeting the behavioral demands and performance conditions of previous jobs and assignments. Candidates are asked to give descriptions of specific situations and their actual behavior in handling them. The interviews are recorded and transcribed for analysis.

Instrumented assessments, such as the California Psychological Inventory[24] are completed by the candidates and used to enrich the analysis of job-person match.

Analysis

Interview transcripts are content-analyzed to determine the types of situations with which candidates have experience and their characteristic patterns of behavior in responding to job situations and performance conditions. Interview data are combined with the results from instrumented assessment. A profile of personal behavioral attributes is prepared for comparison with the behavioral demands of the job/assignment.

The candidate's actual experience doing the critical aspects of the key executive job you are filling is what is important.

For example, if planning and implementing a deep, cost-cutting initiative is a key requirement, the candidate's experience is critical. It makes a big difference if the candidate has just observed or participated in such an initiative or has actually led the initiative.

Or, as in the Special Technology case, leading the development of a strategy is different from just participating in the process that someone else is leading.

Job/Person Match

The candidates' behavioral profiles are compared with the behavioral profiles of the job/assignment. The degree of fit between

---

[24] Ggugh, H., and Bradley, P. *CPI 260® Manual.* Mountain View, CA: COO, Inc. 2005.

person and job is a direct measure of the risk of placing a given candidate in the job.

- Candidates who fit the job/assignment well have a high probability of success and are a low risk.

- Candidates who are close to meeting but fall short on one or more critical demands of the job have a lower probability of success and represent moderate risk.

- Candidates whose profiles do not match the job with regard to one or more critical factors have a low probability of success and are considered to be high risk for the job.

A perfect match is rarely achieved. However, the job/person matching process is very helpful in clarifying the tradeoffs made when choosing among two or more candidates for a job. If only one candidate is being considered, this process will inform the decision to offer the job to the candidate or to keep looking.

Through job/person matching, decision-makers become explicitly aware of the tradeoffs they are making by choosing one candidate over another. They are also able to identify areas in which the candidate(s) may require additional support to succeed in the assignment.

Using an executive job/person matching process is a highly effective approach for enhancing the success of selection decisions for key positions and assignments. In the case of Andy F., an executive job/person match assessment would have revealed the discrepancies between Andy's personal attributes and the job demands of the CEO of Special Technology Inc. described above. Despite looking exceptionally good on paper and interviewing very well, Andy would have been identified as a high-risk candidate for the job.

Next, we will turn to leadership development, which is a key process for ensuring that you have the right people to fill important leadership roles.

Developing People for Key Leadership Positions

The path to becoming a highly effective leader requires:

- Complexity capability

- Heart

- Awareness

- Knowledge

- Skill

Complexity Capability

Over the course of my career, I have worked with CEOs, senior executives, and mid-level managers in companies that range from startups to the Fortune 100. As the case of Andy F. presented above illustrates, one of the most important and fundamental characteristics of people being groomed for and selected into key roles is the degree to which their cognitive capability for complexity matches the complexity of the role or position.[25]

The complexity of the CEO's role in an early stage startup is significantly less than that of a midsized growth company, which is significantly less than that of a large, global enterprise, such as Ford,

---

[25] See: Jaques, Elliott and Cason, Kathryn. *Human Capability: A Study of Individual Potential and Its Application.* Falls Church, VA: Cason Hall & Co. Publishers Limited, 1994.

IBM, or Boeing. One of the key elements of success is the person's complexity capability, his/her ability to create a sound plan that addresses the complexity of the situation and execute it to achieve a desired result within a specified time.

One of the aspects of company evolution, which I have observed consistently, is that as a company grows its complexity grows exponentially. The complexity of roles, especially at senior levels, frequently outgrows the capability of the person who occupies the role.

By moving people through roles of increasing complexity, you can both grow them and test their capability to handle complexity. Be careful of moving people into roles where there are significant gaps between the complexity of their current assignments and the role you are trying to staff. Most people grow best by stretching their capabilities rather than being thrown into situations that are way over their heads—although people with very high complexity capability have the best chance of surviving a severe mismatch.

Heart

By heart, I mean an earnest desire to become an effective leader. Over the course of my career, I have worked with, trained, and mentored several thousand leaders. I have learned that becoming a leader requires a willingness to be open to learning and feedback.

Awareness

Developing yourself or others to be effective leaders requires leadership awareness. Leadership awareness requires us to be mindful of thoughts, feelings, and actions in the situations in which we find ourselves.

Awareness of our actions as leaders and their impact on ourselves and others is of particular importance. When we are mindful as leaders, we are aware of what we are doing and open to information from others about the results of our actions.

Developing leadership awareness is facilitated by exposure to role models who are themselves effective leaders. One of the key aspects of your and your team's leadership is to be role models for the aspiring leaders in your organization.

This brings us back to the importance of daily leadership behavior. Remember that daily behavior is the currency of leadership. Your aspiring leaders are observing you and the members of your team. It is natural for them to emulate the behavior they observe whether it is good leadership or bad.

Mentoring and coaching are other critical sources of leadership awareness. You and other executives are in a position to observe and provide timely feedback to developing leaders. This is yet another area that can be uncomfortable if the person has one or more serious deficiencies that are detracting from their capability to meet the requirements of their role. Again, if you or other senior leaders will not step up to it, who will?

Knowledge

Effective leadership requires knowledge of what to do in the many situations a leader may face. These range from the fundamentals of leading a team on a daily basis to providing strategic leadership for an entire organization.

While formal leadership training programs can be helpful, the fact is that most leadership development happens on the job. The impact of role models, coaching, and mentoring cannot be over emphasized.

Knowledge is not enough, however. Leadership is an active discipline. It requires skill to put knowledge into action.

Skill

Doing is the essence of becoming skillful at anything. To develop leadership capabilities requires placing a person in situations where he/she has the opportunity to lead.

This is where heart, or the earnest desire to become an effective leader, is challenged and tested. Mastering any new behavior or situation requires us to be open to discomfort and feedback. We normally start out by being clumsy at the new behavior. In a good learning environment, we get timely feedback about the effectiveness of our behavior, support for our effort, suggestions for improvement, and repeated opportunities to practice and perfect our skill.

Again, effective mentoring and coaching are indispensable to creating an effective learning environment. As is practice, practice, practice!

> **Practice doesn't make perfect. Perfect practice makes perfect.—Yogi Berra**

One of the outcomes of highly effective strategic leadership is a corporate culture that supports sustained high performance at the unit and team levels.

Chapter 7:
High-Performance Culture

Culture is a company's core social environment. It is comprised of the norms, values, expectations, beliefs, and behaviors of people in the organization. It affects the organization's performance by consistently supporting high performance or serving as an impediment to it.

I first encountered a high-performance organization culture when I reported for summer practice at The Ohio State University. It was the summer of 1963. Woody Hayes had won the National Championship in 1961.

From the first day of camp, it was clear that Woody was all about playing at a championship level. Our mission was to win the Big Ten Conference Championship and above all to beat Michigan.

The focus was on quality and performance in every aspect of championship level play, from the quality of the players and coaching staff, to recruiting, to preparation on and off the practice field, to our academic performance. To this day, it is the only situation in which my performance was filmed and scored at every practice and game.

After four years of Ohio State football, I was deeply experienced with how a high-performance organization worked.

When you look at teams that have sustained championship level play over an extended number of years, such as the Ohio State Buckeyes, the Alabama Crimson Tide, the Golden State Warriors, the New England Patriots, and the US Women's Soccer Team, you will find superior leadership emanating from the team's CEO, the head coach.

An excellent introduction to the importance of leadership to the maintenance of high-performance culture is the book *Sea Stories* by Admiral William McRaven.[26] In it, McRaven gives many examples of how central command leadership is to sustain the Special Operations culture.

Your company culture results from the dynamic interplay of strategy, structure, systems, jobs, people, and leadership. It takes form in the daily behavior of executives, managers, and employees. High-performance organizations have strong cultures that explicitly express values and behaviors that are critical for sustaining high performance. A high-performance corporate culture includes the following key elements:

- **Performance**. A high-performance culture encourages people to perform at their best and to improve performance continually. Performance expectations are clear. People have to perform well to keep their jobs. A track record of effective performance is a requirement for promotion. Reward systems tie recognition and appreciation directly to performance. The core leadership helps establish performance standards for all jobs and provides the support people need to meet those job expectations. Effective compensation practices tie compensation to capability and performance.

- **Quality.** Leadership in a high-performance organization constantly looks for, finds, and rewards quality. Continuous improvement in quality is the sum of many small steps over time. For this reason, every employee must understand and support the organization's strategic focus.

---

[26]McRaven, William H., *Sea Stories: My Life In Special Operations.*

By emphasizing the importance of producing superior-quality work in all facets of its operations and recognizing people's contributions to quality, the high-performance organization builds pride in quality into its culture. The core leadership makes quality an explicit key value, defining quality criteria and standards for all key business processes and developing measurements to track quality over time.

For example, a company might use interviews, focus groups, and survey questionnaires to assess customers' perceptions of the organization's products and services. Employees can then use this information to review service issues with the customers and to assure that each customer receives a superior level of service.

- **People.** High-performance organizations go beyond the platitude that "people are our most important resource" to actually value people, respect them, and treat them fairly. Through core values and management practices and processes, the leadership views and treats people as partners in the business.

  When managers take actions that affect people, they pursue fair treatment and demonstrate a genuine concern for their well-being. Top management solicits employees' opinions on issues that affect them and offers honest information, before implementation, about such issues as pay, performance, and job security.

- **Communication.** Among an organization's greatest resources are the knowledge and experience of its people. To make this knowledge and experience accessible to those who need it, high-performance organizations foster extensive networking.

Communications flow freely—up, down, laterally, and diagonally. People have access to the information they need to do their jobs and communicate freely across organizational lines.

Senior managers are interested in and available to people. Through breakfast meetings and focus groups with employees, employee meetings, and a lot of walking around, the core leadership stays close to employees and demonstrates a genuine concern for effective communication. The feedback loops that grow out of this open communication promote organizational learning.

- **Participation.** Building commitment to the organization through involvement is a key characteristic of high-performance cultures. People participate actively in solving work-related problems and making decisions that affect them. Extensive use of teams involves the people responsible for implementation in problem solving, planning, and design.

- **Managerial leadership.** In addition to building effective leadership networks, high-performance organizations focus explicitly on managerial leadership. The core leadership expects managers at all levels to set good examples in all their actions and encourages them to speak out on issues, support their people, set direction for their areas of responsibility, and take appropriate risks.

The organization has explicit standards of excellence for managers, and managers receive the training, mentoring, and coaching required to develop the high-performance management behaviors they need to meet the standards.

The standards for managers are key factors in performance appraisals and compensation.

- **Adaptability.** Change is an important aspect of organizational life. Organizations that fail to recognize the need for change, or fail to act on it, imperil their survival.

  In high-performance organizations, anticipation of and responsiveness to change are explicit values in their cultures. These organizations maintain close relationships with customers, suppliers, and industry organizations to stay in touch with the changing business environment.

  The core leadership sees change as the normal course of business. Management and employees continuously scan the environment, recognize the need for change quickly, make necessary changes smoothly and efficiently, and meet people's needs for support when changes occur.

- **Innovation.** Organizations that stand still, continuing to operate the way they always have, will fall behind in today's fast-paced and ever-changing business world. High-performance organizations encourage people to take risks and try new ways of doing things to improve work processes, products, and services. By continuously pushing the envelope on processes, products, and services, high-performance organizations maintain a continuous state of learning and self-renewal.

Learning Organization

High-performance companies are learning organizations. They gain knowledge or understanding through study or instruction and modify their behaviors through experience and anticipation.

Individual learning is a prerequisite for organizational learning. To foster learning, high-performance organizations build environments that value personal and team learning, encourage the development of collaboration skills, promote risk-taking, and explore failures. They also provide feedback loops through communication systems, evaluation criteria, and open dialog.

In both personal and organizational learning, some "unlearning" must take place before the true learning begins and takes hold. Organizational unlearning calls for rigorous examination of existing assumptions, beliefs, rules, and myths. Often, learning takes place only after people fully let go of these assumptions. Active learning is a continual cycle that moves from unlearning to learning to unlearning to learning.

A learning organization is effective when a clear strategic focus provides a context and purpose for learning. Otherwise, an organization may pursue learning for learning's sake and fail in business.[27]

Building and sustaining a high-performance culture creates the conditions for highly effective unit and team leadership.

---

[27] For a thorough description of learning organizations, see Senge, Peter M. *The Fifth Discipline: The Art & Practice of the Learning Organization*. New York: Doubleday, 2006.

Chapter 8:
Highly Effective Unit and Team Leadership

A highly effective executive team is a necessary but not a sufficient condition for building a high-performance organization. The senior leadership sets the direction and leads the execution. However, the real work is in units and teams. The larger the organization, the more units and teams are required to get the work done. A key part of your and the senior team's job is to assure that there is abundant high-performance leadership of the units and teams in your organization.

Units and teams are the basic building blocks of every organization. In today's complex, ever-changing, and fast-paced business environment, the actual work of an organization gets done by groups of people organized into units and teams. The type and quality of leadership drives performance at the unit and team level. This then becomes a critical factor that determines how well or poorly an organization will perform.

Units and teams are both organizations of people designed to get something done. Units usually have a long-life expectancy. They are formal organizational elements consisting of a number of people over whom a manager has direct authority and responsibility.

Teams normally have a limited life cycle. A team leader, who frequently has no direct managerial authority or responsibility over team members, heads a team. Team members represent various organizational functions and are typically drawn together to do a specific piece of work. From a leadership perspective, once a team is formed there is little difference between the behaviors required of a team leader and those required of a unit leader when it comes to producing high performance.

One of the keys to achieving and sustaining high performance at the company level is to build an organization with an abundance of high-performing units and teams. There are two critical elements that differentiate high-performing units and teams from moderate and low-performing teams and units: they are the climate or work environment of the unit and the leadership behavior of the unit leader.

Unit/Team Climate

Every unit, team, and work group establishes a climate, a work environment that persists from day to day. It exists in the perceptions of unit and team members. Research of organizations ranging from engineering groups to nuclear submarine crews, consistently shows that unit climate is the factor that explains the difference between high, moderate, and low performance.

Spend some time in a unit or team and you will begin to sense the climate in which the members are working. If you visit a high-performance unit, you will notice there is a purposeful "hum" throughout the unit. Work is getting done and people are focused and full of positive energy. When people get together, they focus on solving problems and finding ways to do their work more effectively.

A trip to a moderate or low-performance unit reveals a different story. You can feel a tension in the air. People are working hard but there is no joy in it. When people get together it is more likely that they are complaining to one another about having to work overtime or about the latest change in the project rather than working to solve a problem or do their work more effectively.

Research into high-performing units has isolated six climate factors that differentiate them from moderate and low-performing units: clarity, commitment, excellence, responsibility, recognition, and teamwork.[28]

1. **Clarity** is the degree to which unit members understand expectations, goals, policies, and job requirements, and perceive that things run smoothly.

2. **Commitment** is the degree to which people are committed to achieving the unit's goals and the extent to which they continually use goals to evaluate their own performance.

3. **Excellence** is the emphasis that managers and unit members place on setting high standards of performance and continuously improving performance.

4. **Responsibility** is the degree to which team members feel they are personally responsible for their work and they are encouraged to take initiative in solving problems and getting things done.

5. **Recognition** is the degree to which members perceive they are recognized and rewarded for doing good work.

6. **Teamwork** is the degree to which members perceive they are part of a team, take pride in belonging to the work unit, and support each other.

Leader Behavior

Daily behavior is the currency of leadership. It drowns out words and drives unit and team climate. A unit leader is highly visible to the

---

[28] Burgin, A. Lad. *Leading Units and Teams for High Performance*. HRMG-LLC, 2017 (available at hrmg-llc.com).

people she/he leads. Even apparently insignificant behavior can have a strong impact on employees.

A leadership style is a set of related behaviors that a leader uses to influence people to perform. Some leadership styles contribute to a high-performance climate, while other styles detract from it. Research into high-performance units and teams has identified six types of leadership behavior.[29] Three of these, Pace Setting, Social, and Coercive detract from unit and team climate. The three other types, Directive, Participative, and Coaching, are the primary drivers of a high-performance climate.

1. **Pace Setting**. There are both positive and negative aspects to this style. The positive is that a leader who uses this style leads by example. Through her personal actions she demonstrates high personal standards and commitment.

   The negative aspect is that she expects her direct reports to perform effectively with little support from her. She is often unwilling to trust important tasks and projects to others and gets personally involved. When performance fails to meet her expectations, she becomes very critical. She believes that "People should motivate themselves and not require pats on the back."

   Pace setting leaders rely on this style when things are going well. When things are not going well, they have a pronounced tendency to become coercive.

---

[29] Burgin, A. Lad. *Leading Units and Teams for High Performance*. HRMG-LLC, 2017 (available at hrmg-llc.com).

2. **Social**. A leader using the social style tries to build warm and friendly relationships with his direct reports and others. He is highly likely to put people ahead of performance, withhold negative feedback, smooth over conflict, and put people's feelings and happiness ahead of task accomplishment.

   A moderate amount of this style can be helpful. When it is overused, it negatively impacts clarity, excellence, responsibility, and recognition. Highly social leaders most often engender a high level of commitment to them rather than to the unit and its performance.

3. **Coercive**. A leader using the coercive style dictates exactly what and how things will be done. She expects her direct reports to follow her decisions with little or no discussion. She wants things done her way. She relies heavily on negative feedback and personal criticism to control performance. She tries to motivate people by threatening to withhold something of value to them, such as, "If you want that raise, you better get this done."

   This style can be effective in specific situations when it is necessary to get the attention of an individual or an entire unit. When it is over-used, it has a negative impact on commitment, responsibility, recognition, and teamwork.

4. **Directive**. A leader using the directive style sets clear goals and expectations. He will be tactful but leave no doubt that he is in charge. He solicits input from the people involved before making decisions. He takes the time to explain the reasons behind his directions and decisions and ties them to the interests of the organization and the team members. He monitors performance and lets people know if they have done well or missed the mark. He relies primarily on positive

feedback to manage performance but does use negative feedback when appropriate.

5. **Participative.** A leader using this style relies on participation to get people involved and build commitment. She delegates important tasks and projects to people and lets them run with them. She brings her staff and teams of people together to collaborate in setting goals, making plans, and solving problems. She encourages participation by team members in making decisions. She emphasizes teamwork and recognizes team performance more than individual contributions.

6. **Coaching.** A leader using the coaching style continually works with individuals and teams to develop their capabilities. He asks his direct reports to set their own performance goals and plans to support the unit's goals. He expects people to identify problems and suggest solutions. He takes time to show people how they can improve their performance. He observes and reviews performance and provides constructive feedback. He gives people as much authority and responsibility as they can handle and recognizes them for effective performance.

If you spend some time observing the behavior of high-performance unit and team leaders, you will see that they use direction, participation, and coaching with a dash of pace setting and social in an effective blend of leadership styles that meet the needs of a situation. Lower-performance leaders rely on the pace setting, social, and coercive styles and underutilize the high-performance styles.

Daily leadership behaviors drive climate. Reliance on the pace setting, social, and coercive styles undermines unit and team climate and performance. Mastery of the directive, participative, and coaching styles produces and sustains a high-performance climate. High unit climate results in high performance.

In leadership transitions, it can take six months, or more, of consistent, high-performance leadership to shift a low-performance unit climate to a high-performance unit climate. Likewise, a high-performance unit climate can be ruined in six months by ineffective unit leadership.

If your interest is in developing high-performance leadership in your organization, there are also several things to focus on:

1. The first is your own behavior. Behavior modeled by key leaders has a very strong impact on other leaders in an organization.

2. Pay attention to climate and leadership. Explicitly evaluate leaders on their leadership behavior and the climate they create for their people.

3. Provide a process for leaders to develop and maintain their leadership skills. Once again, mentoring and coaching are critically important.

4. Don't tolerate consistently poor leadership. Leaving people who have demonstrated they are not interested and/or not capable of leading effectively in leadership positions undermines leaders who are striving to lead well. It compromises performance and is ultimately unfair to the people reporting to the ineffective leaders.

5. Make demonstrated capability of high-performance leadership a critical selection criterion for key management positions.

A high level of leadership at the unit/team level sets the stage to carry the business agenda into execution by focusing on results at the individual and team levels.

Chapter 9:
Focus on Results

Bill, CEO of a large information technology company, asked me to come by for a cup of coffee. As we met, I learned that Bill was concerned about improving the performance of his company. He wanted to know what I thought about his management team and what the steps should be to take the company to the next level.

I replied that the thing that struck me about his management team was the lack of discipline in their thinking about performance. From the interactions I'd had with them, it was clear to me that the members of the team lacked a common language for talking about performance issues and had no common, rigorous process for defining the results they were trying to achieve and holding their people accountable for their accomplishment.

Bill thought for a few moments. He then asked me what I thought a good performance management process would look like.

I replied that companies that did a really good job of performance management had several things in common. They effectively:

- Set clear expectations.

- Focus on results.

- Monitor status.

- Review results.

- Hold people accountable.

Clear Expectations

By clear expectations, I mean that people throughout these companies know they have to be good at what they do if they want to continue with these companies. Just performing at a moderate level is not acceptable. Leaders in these companies set the bar at a level that is both challenging and achievable and expect people to perform at that level. Leaders are expected to provide reasonable support to assist people to perform above the bar, but the basic rule is "be good or be gone."

Focus on Results

A result is best described as "what by when." What is going to be accomplished in specific, observable terms by what date.

In high-performance companies, results drive peoples' behavior. Each person in the organization understands his or her job in terms of its Key Performance Areas (KPAs) and Key Performance Indicators (KPIs).

- **Key Performance Areas**. In these companies, managers and employees have mastered the capability to take a job or assignment and break it down into three to seven Key Performance Areas. Each KPA represents a major chunk of the job. For example, a typical CEO's job has the following KPAs:

    o   Building customer relationships.

    o   Working with the board.

    o   Developing strategy and positioning the business.

    o   Leading the company.

o Operational execution.

o Communicating with stakeholders, such as customers, employees, shareholders, investment analysts, the community, etc.

Each person is responsible for defining the Key Performance Indicators for each KPA.

- **Key Performance Indicators**. A second capability that is highly developed in high-performance organizations is the development of Key Performance Indicators for each Key Performance Area. These are the "what by when's." They are specific statements describing the result to be accomplished and the target date for its accomplishment. Here are two examples of KPIs for a CEO:

  o Building customer relationships—establish a plan and implement two customer visits per year with each major customer.

  o Working with the board—advise all board members of any issues that may have a substantial impact on business strategy, operational execution, or stakeholder relationships within five days of becoming aware of them.

One very popular approach to developing KPAs and KPIs is the Balanced Scorecard developed by Robert Kaplan and David Norton.[30]

An effective process of results setting and review is essential to building high performance into a company's culture. At the beginning

---

[30] Kaplan, Robert S. and Norton, David P. *The Balanced Scorecard: Translating Strategy into Action*. Boston: Harvard Business School Press, 1996.

of the process, each person drafts his/her performance plan for the performance period. A performance period may be as short as a month for some positions and as long as several years for others. It all depends on the nature of the job or assignment.

The performance plan is organized by Key Performance Areas, and Key Performance Indicators are specified for each KPA. In most highly effective processes, there is a period of iteration as people formulate their performance plans and review them with their managers and colleagues. At a designated point in time, everyone is expected to have a finalized performance plan.

Monitoring Status

Honesty and integrity are the key elements for monitoring status. Reporting the status of key initiatives and objectives requires a commitment by each team member to "tell it like it is."

I have used several approaches to monitoring performance against plan. The one I like the best is the simple green, yellow, and red color system.

Please come prepared to update the team on progress on your key objectives and any additions or other changes. Please use the following to report on the status of each objective:

Green – There is a **valid plan** to achieve the objective and it is **on schedule.**

Yellow – There is a **valid plan** to achieve the objective and it is **behind schedule.**

Red – There is a **no valid plan** to achieve the objective.

This system provides a clear way to track any number of initiatives and objectives. It facilitates team business review meetings that keep all the team members engaged and accountable for results.

Review

A rigorous review process is an integral part of building and maintaining an effective focus on results and a high level of teamwork. Performance plans become the basis for a weekly business review. In the best processes, performance plans are living documents. People use the performance plans to record their progress, show current status of KPIs, and capture results as they are achieved. When progress on KPIs is behind plan or the plan is no longer valid, the person is responsible for alerting the team and for getting back on track.

With mutual consent of the person and his or her manager, the performance plan is adjusted to accurately reflect what is happening in their day-to-day execution. KPIs may be added, or dropped, or target completion dates may be modified as business circumstances change. The performance plan is a living document that becomes the basis for accountability.

Accountability

Accountability comes from having to sit with your manager, the management team, or the board and review the results that you are actually achieving or have achieved with respect to your performance plan. In most cases, some results will have been achieved and some will have been missed. In high-performance companies, most of the results on the plan will be achieved. Appropriate recognition and rewards go to those who consistently achieve results. Plans to improve achievement are developed for those who fall short of achieving the results that define their performance. Those who consistently fail to achieve are asked to pursue their careers elsewhere.

Bill and I kicked these ideas around for a while. We concluded that he needed to implement a thorough review of his company's performance-management business process as the next step in his overall initiative to improve performance.

Building and sustaining a high-performance company requires strong, strategic leadership. Sustaining strong, strategic leadership over an extended period requires an effective leadership practice.

Chapter 10.
Sustaining the Capacity to Lead:
Building an Effective Leadership Practice

Strategic leadership is the process of attracting, energizing, focusing, aligning, and retaining people to accomplish results and build a high-performance organization.

It takes energy to be an effective leader. An executive must develop and maintain the capacity to lead. He/she must be physically, mentally, and emotionally available.

High capacity leaders are focused, act purposefully to address situations, and set the positive example required to maintain the performance of an organization. Leaders who allow themselves to become tired or overly stressed become reactive, lose focus, and have difficulty enacting and sustaining the daily behavior required to lead effectively.

The path to sustained, effective leadership involves a practice of thinking, feeling, and acting on a daily basis.

Leadership Is a Journey

Leading an organization of any scale is full of victories and defeats, and problems and challenges. If you are in an unfortunate situation, there may even be one or more catastrophes along the way. Executive leadership is a journey that happens and is revealed to us one day at a time. Today may be pleasing and tomorrow dreadful. This is the reality of the world in which leaders live.

At the end of the journey, the effectiveness of your leadership will be defined by thousands of decisions and actions taken on a daily basis. Each of us compiles a body of work on our leadership journey.

The greatest asset we can have in building our body of work is mindfulness.

Mindfulness

To be mindful is to be aware of thoughts, feelings, and actions in the situations in which we find ourselves. Mindfulness of our actions and their impact on ourselves and others is of particular importance. When we are mindful, we are aware of what we are doing and open to information from others about the results of our actions.

Mindfulness allows us to be aware of whether our actions are harmful or helpful to ourselves and others. To me, two of the fundamental measures of effective leadership are harm and help.

Harm and Help

How much harm have I done to myself and others through my daily actions? It is difficult, if not impossible, to go through a leadership journey without causing some harm. However, approaching each situation in each day with the intention of not doing harm puts us squarely on the path to effective leadership.

Mindfulness allows us to be aware when we are engaging in thoughts, feelings, and actions that are harmful to ourselves or others. It allows us to cease harmful ways and make amends for harm we have caused. Being mindful about harm allows us to build a body of work in which we have minimized the harm we have done. First, do no harm!

How much help have I provided to myself and others through my daily actions? For me, the second and perhaps most important measure of a leader's body of work is the amount of help that one has given to one's self and others.

I include one's self because our relationship to ourselves is a major contributor to the quality of our leadership. If I am helpful to myself, I treat myself with respect and care for my mental, emotional, and physical well-being. If I am helpful to others, I treat them with respect and care for their well-being.

In summing up a leader's body of work in terms of both intention and result, does the help given outweigh the harm done. To build a body of leadership work in which you help when and if you can, and do no harm, requires a mindful approach to daily leadership. It requires a practice.

Practice

A practice is a set of activities that a person does repeatedly to attain and sustain proficiency at something. Effective leadership unfolds one day at a time through mindful thinking, feeling, and acting. Achieving and sustaining the capacity to lead requires a daily leadership practice. These are some key aspects of my practice:

- Intention and action

- Meditation

- Exercise, nutrition, and sleep

- Gratitude

- Relationships

- Adventure

Intention and action are starting points for daily practice. Starting the day with a clear intention as to how we would like it to be and following through with appropriate action is at the heart of practice. In fashioning a leadership practice, we must come to grips with this question:

When I interact with others, what do I want them to take away from the interaction?

There are many choices. Your interactions with others can leave them feeling positive, respected, valued, and appreciated. Or, their experience of you can leave them frightened, frustrated, angry, demeaned, or unappreciated.

If we were walking together through your organization, what would I see when you encountered people?

- Would they approach you, or find a way to escape interacting with you?

- Would they be energized from interacting with you, or would they be demoralized, or frightened?

- Would they answer your questions honestly, or tell you what they think you want to hear?

For me, the capacity to lead embodies mindful daily thinking, feeling, and acting, in accordance with some basic precepts:

- Calm in approaching the trials and challenges of daily leadership

- Focus on results

- Balance in my daily activities among work, family, friends, personal time, and recreation

- Harmony in my relationships with myself and others

- Compassion for others and their life situations and challenges

- Joy and gratitude for the many good things in my life

- Love for the people in my life

- Kindness to the people with whom I interact

Starting each day with the intention to implement these things sets the stage for a "good day." When I finish the day having engaged in them, I find I am pleased with the day even if it has been difficult and I am not satisfied by all that has taken place.

Meditation is the key to a calm mind. At some point in my journey, I discovered that life is much more satisfying when it is encountered with a calm mind. In my work and in my personal life, I have experienced many times that things just work better when my mind is calm, and I am centered.

This is particularly true when leading others. Approaching daily challenges and situations with calmness, focus, and proactivity fosters confidence in the people experiencing your leadership. Approaching situations with anxiety, anger, frustration, or aggression fosters fear and defensiveness.

I find that daily meditation allows me to remain calm and centered when working through whatever comes up during the day. Therefore, I have incorporated a twenty-minute meditation into my practice. My intention is to meditate every day and my action is to do it most days. If I can't manage twenty minutes, ten minutes is still significant. I have found there are many times during a day when one can use an otherwise idle time to meditate, such as when stuck in traffic, or if someone is late for an appointment.

Exercise, nutrition, and sleep are essential to maintaining personal well-being and the capacity to lead. Effective leadership takes alertness and energy. By adopting and acting on an intention of eating a good diet, getting regular, aerobic exercise, and sleeping for at least eight hours each night, we are able to be at, or near, our best each day. We have the energy to meet leadership's challenges and opportunities.

Good nutrition involves not only eating a good diet, but avoiding overindulgence in alcohol and caffeine, and not using drugs. Aerobic exercise can range from walking, to bicycling, to running, or my favorite—an orbital cross trainer. Regular exercise several times a week is what is important. Getting a good night's sleep is essential to being able to function well physically, emotionally, and mentally. In my experience, a leader who is operating with serious sleep deprivation lacks the capacity to be mindful and calm.

Gratitude is the engine of emotional well-being. Gratitude is the awareness and appreciation of the good people and things in our lives.

We all visit two different emotional realms. There is the Realm of Positive Emotions, such as joy, love, awe, and enthusiasm. And, there is the Realm of Negative Emotions, such as envy, hate, fear, anger, frustration, and sadness. Every day, we each make a choice of which emotional realm we will visit. If we consistently visit the same realm, we eventually become a resident there.

It is hard for me to conceive of leading effectively while residing in the Realm of Negative Emotions. The people I know who live there are unhappy, depressed, and not pleasant to be around. They drive the people they are trying to lead into the Negative Realm. The Realm of Positive Emotions is the source of effective leadership. This is where gratitude comes in.

When we stop and think about, or write down things for which we are grateful, we take ourselves to the Realm of Positive Emotions and we strengthen the positive circuits in our brains. When we dwell on the things and people we don't like, the things we don't have, and the troubles we face, we visit the Negative Realm and strengthen these circuits. Putting gratitude into our daily leadership practice keeps us a resident in the Realm of Positive Emotions. We may be drawn to the negative from time to time, but gratitude will bring us back to the positive.

Relationships appear to be what matters most as we look at our lives. Deep satisfaction comes from being in meaningful relationships with family and friends. Loneliness and isolation accrue to those who are disconnected from others. When George Vaillant, the curator of the long-term Harvard Grant Study,[31] was asked to sum-up what he had learned about satisfaction with life from following the study participants over many years, he answered:

"The only thing that really matters in life is your relationships to other people."

It is much easier to sustain our effectiveness as leaders if we have the support of friends and family members. In my work as a business advisor to senior executives, I have had the opportunity to talk with many executives as they approached the end of their carriers. Their biggest regret has consistently been that they put too much time and effort into their work and not enough time and effort into their relationships with spouses, children, and friends.

Relationships don't just happen. They require time and energy and attention. As with the other aspects of effective leadership, building and maintaining meaningful relationships takes both intention and action.

Adventure adds spice to life. A sense of adventure, what in Aikido is called the "mind of the beginner," allows us to see the opportunities that surround us. It opens us up to new experiences. It generates enthusiasm and zest for life. A leader without enthusiasm drains energy from people. A leader with a strong sense of adventure energizes others.

I have found that cultivating and incorporating a sense of adventure into my practice is a great source of pleasure and satisfaction.

To help me focus my intention and action, I begin each day by reading a poem I wrote, which was inspired by Mary Oliver's "Messenger."[32]

---

[31] "What Makes Us Happy?" by Joshua Wolf Shenk, 2009, *The Atlantic Online*, June 2009.

[32] *Thirst: Poems*. Boston: Beacon Press, 2006.

Awakening

Today I awakened to the opportunity of a new day.
My life is an adventure.
I journey mindfully.
What astonishing things will I encounter today?

The Value of Practice

My practice has become an integral part of my daily life. It keeps me calm, centered, focused, and balanced. It helps me to enjoy each day. Its value became particularly clear to me in September of 2010 when my oldest son died suddenly and unexpectedly.

My practice helped me navigate the grief and sadness. It enabled me to hold onto and appreciate the many blessings in my life. It helped me to heal. It enabled me to continue to lead effectively.

We practice every day to sustain our effectiveness as leaders. When difficulty or tragedy strikes, our practice allows us to lean into it and move through it. It allows us to endure great stress without suffering.

I hope you find this helpful as you think about your own life and develop your own leadership practice.

What astonishing things will you encounter today?

An organization that develops an abundance of high-performance leaders and couples them to the elements of a clear strategic focus, right structure, right people, high-performance culture, and a focus on results harnesses the energy of the organization's people and achieves a competitive advantage that is difficult and costly to duplicate.

Bibliography

Bossidy, Larry and Charan, Ram. *Execution: The Discipline of Getting Things Done.* New York: Crown Business, 2002.

Burgin, A. Lad and Koss, Ellee. *Transformation to High Performance: A journey in organizational learning.* SRI International Business Intelligence Program, Report 823 (Summer 1993).

Burgin, A. Lad. "Leading Units and Teams for High Performance." HRMG-LLC, 2017.

Collins, James C. *Good to Great.* New York: Harper Collins Publishers, 2001.

Collins, James C. and Porras, Jerry I. *Built to Last.* New York: Harper Collins Publishers, 1994.

Gerstner, Louis V., Jr. *Who Says Elephants Can't Dance?* New York: Harper Collins Publishers, 2002.

Ggugh, H., and Bradley, P. *CPI 260® Manual.* Mountain View, CA: COO, Inc. 2005.

Hoffman, Bryce G. *American Icon: Alan Mulally and the Fight to Save Ford Motor Company.* New York: Currency Books, 2012.

Jaques, Elliott, *Requisite Organization.* Arlington, VA: CASON Hall, 1998.

Jaques, Elliott, *Social Power and the CEO: Leadership and Trust in a Sustainable Free Enterprise System.* Westport, CT: Quorum Books, 2002.

Jaques, Elliott and Cason, Kathryn. *Human Capability: A Study of Individual Potential and Its Application.* Falls Church, VA: Cason Hall & Co. Publishers Limited, 1994.

Kaplan, Robert S. and Norton, David P. *The Balanced Scorecard: Translating Strategy into Action.* Boston: Harvard Business School Press, 1996.

McCracken, Harry. https://www.fastcompany.com/90331689/amazons-wild-24-year-ride-from-11-employees-to-600000-plus, April 11, 2019.

McRaven, Admiral William H. *Sea Stories: My Life in Special Operations.* New York: Hachette Book Group, Inc., 2019.

Mulally, Alan. CEO of Ford Motor Company interviewed by Charlie Rose 07/27/2011 (https://charlierose.com/videos/15706).

Oliver, Marry. Thirst: Poems. Boston: Beacon Press, 2006.

Senge, Peter M. *The Fifth Discipline: The Art & Practice of the Learning Organization*. New York: Doubleday, 2006.

Thurow, Lester. *The Future of Capitalism*. New York: William Morrow and Company, 1996.

Kennedy, John F. Speech to Congress delivered May 25, 1961.

Shenk Joshua Wolf., "What Makes Us Happy?", *The Atlantic Online*, June 2009.

About the Author

Lad Burgin is the President and CEO of HRMG, LLC., a management consulting firm that provides business, organizational, and leadership effectiveness services. For more than forty years, Lad has worked as a business executive and a consultant to other business executives and their teams. His previous positions include: Executive Consultant at Informix Software; President and CEO of Gynecare, Inc. (publicly traded); President and CEO of the Benefits Systems Division of the Transamerica Life Companies; Corporate Vice President Human Resources and Director of Management Development with Transamerica Corporation; and Manager of Advanced Management Development Programs with SCM Corporation.

Lad is recognized internationally for his work with CEOs, their teams and boards. He has consulted with executives in more than 300 companies in twenty-five different industries around the world. He has served on the Board of Directors with five companies and has consulted with Boards to improve their effectiveness. He has worked with companies ranging in size from Silicon Valley start-ups to the top Fortune 100. His clients have included: 3Com, Bank of America, Boston Scientific, Charles Schwab, Dynavax, Hansen Medical, Simplex Solutions, Sunesis Pharmaceuticals, Synergy Semiconductor, Triton Container, Visa, Voyage Medical, Hewlett Packard, Informix Software, International Asset Systems, Legato Systems, McKesson, and Molecular Devices.

Lad's consulting focus is working with executives as a confidential advisor and coach to help build and sustain high performance. His expertise includes business strategy design and execution, key executive selection, executive team and board of director effectiveness, strategic organizational change and transformation, and executive leadership development and succession planning.

Lad is the author of "The Power of Executive Leadership," "Leading Units and Teams for High Performance," and "Making Mergers Work," published by HRMG, LLC. He is also the coauthor of "Transformation to High Performance," published by SRI International (Summer 1993), and "Orchestrating the Renewal: Creating and Maintaining a High-Performance Board," published in *Directors and Boards* (Spring 1994). His writing can be found on his leadership website L4HP.com.

Lad is an avid sailor and can be found in his spare time either working on his 40-foot ketch, *Shadowside*, or sailing out of Port Hadlock, WA. In 2016 he sailed the *Shadowside* from San Francisco to Hawaii and then on to Port Townsend, WA.

Lad is a graduate of The Ohio State University where he earned B.Sc., MBA, and Ph.D. (Management and Organizational Behavior) degrees and played football for legendary coach Woody Hayes.

www.ingramcontent.com/pod-product-compliance
Lightning Source LLC
Chambersburg PA
CBHW030656220526
45463CB00005B/1806